"Janet Sims has created an accessible yet powerful introduction to the Basic Mindfulness System of meditation pioneer Shinzen Young. Through clear instruction, relevant cases and Janet's own profound depth of experience, you too will be able to select mindfulness methods that meet the challenges of your day, developing your own trusty black bag of mindfulness resources."

- Meg Salter, Integral Master Coach™
MegaSpace Consulting
www.megsalter.com

"As a (mindfulness) practitioner, I appreciate the simplicity and straightforwardness of Janet's presentation; as a mindfulness teacher, I appreciate the elegance and applicability; as a clinician, I enjoy Janet's ability to weave case studies together with a precise, comprehensive, and systematic application of mindfulness training. Janet's *Mindful Awareness and Strategy: A Basic Mindfulness Toolkit* is an excellent guide."

- Todd Mertz,
Business Development Manager
Shinzen Young and Basic Mindfulness

"In *Mindful Awareness and Strategy: A Basic Mindfulness Toolkit*, Dr. Janet Sims achieves a rare feat—a perfect balance between concept and real world application. …As a psychologist who has attended more than one continuing education seminar on mindfulness meditation, I gained a much greater understanding *and* inspiration (for beginning my own meditation practice) from this gem of a book compared to previous books and classes."

- Debbie Hall, Ph.D. clinical psychologist
and co-author of *Relax: Make Stress Work for You; Managing Stress Before It Manages You; Rx for Stress: A Nurse's Guide,* and other works

"I have never practiced mindfulness training and do not have the experience Janet and her students do. I was surprised and so happy that while editing *Mindful Awareness and Strategy: A Basic Mindfulness Toolkit,* I gleaned so many strategies that enabled me to sleep better."

- Samantha Stroh Bailey
Owner, Perfect Pen Communications

"Bursting with simple, but deeply effective exercises, and wise guidance about when and how to use each, Janet points the reader to both acceptance and change."

- Georgia Jones, LCSW
Owner and psychotherapist
Chicago Mindful Therapy and The Mindfulness Clinic

"My pre-teenage daughter who had rarely meditated (that is to say, rarely practiced mindfulness for more than five minutes) stayed with me for a whopping ten minutes when I brought some of Janet's ideas to our meditation. One hundred percent improvement on the first try is auspicious! I definitely feel enthused about bringing the Toolkit to my own students and organizational work with clients. I recommend Janet's Basic Mindfulness Toolkit wholeheartedly."

- Hilary Bradbury, Ph.D., Professor of Organizational Psychology.
Leader in the field of action research and author of the recent acclaimed
Eros/Power: Love in the Spirit of Inquiry

Mindful Awareness and Strategy

A Basic Mindfulness Toolkit

Janet Sims

Foreword

Many people tend to regard mindfulness as esoteric and challenging – a difficult-to-grasp practice with somewhat ambiguous benefits. However, at its essence, mindfulness is quite simply about paying attention. Whether it is paying attention to what is happening inside or around us, mindfulness enables us to be intimately connected to our experience in each moment. In the increasingly disconnected times we find ourselves living, mindfulness is an important tool for staying in contact with what is most vital.

Still, knowing how to get started in mindfulness practice can be intimidating. Even those who are already established practitioners struggle from time to time with how to deepen and expand on what they've already discovered.

As I've found over the years as a mindfulness practitioner and coach, one very effective approach to mindfulness is through the senses – literally what we see, hear, and feel. The senses are such a part of the human experience that most of us can easily relate to them, thus finding a natural, accessible path to cultivating mindful awareness.

Building upon the work of Shinzen Young's, *Basic Mindfulness System*, which emphasizes sensory awareness, Janet Sims has gifted us with a rare book on mindfulness. Janet and I have known each other for several years and worked together both as senior facilitators for Shinzen Young's Home Practice Program and other teaching projects. Combining over a decade of study as a devoted student of Shinzen's with her experience as a mindfulness-based psychotherapist, Janet offers a unique perspective synthesizing all she has learned and discovered along the way.

Mindful Awareness and Strategy: A Basic Mindfulness Toolkit offers a simple, clear, sensory-based approach for understanding mindful awareness; suggests some reasonable goals you might have for developing this type of practice; and perhaps most importantly, provides specific exercises you can immediately implement. Whether you use these exercises yourself or even teach them to someone else, these strategies can be used to manage daily life situations – things as mundane as not overreacting during a disagreement with your partner or friend to dealing with chronic anxiety or fear. In this way, mindfulness becomes extremely practical – something anyone who knows me understands I particularly appreciate.

Having served in several capacities as a helping professional: an oncology nurse, a management development professional, a counselor, a conversational design coach, and a group facilitator, I have had numerous people say to me, "Mindfulness/meditation could probably really help me ... but I just can't do it." What follows is a list of reasons from, "I can't get my mind quiet"; "I don't have enough time to do it"; to "The stuff I have read on mindfulness seems too abstract – too woo-woo."

I tend to view these sentiments as an opportunity – a chance to think about and approach mindfulness in a new way. If you're one of us who struggles with how to get started with mindfulness or deepen your current practice, I'd like to encourage you to think of this book as an experiment in a new way of "doing" mindfulness. Because – at its heart – that's what this book offers: a direct way of tasting and doing mindfulness, not just talking about it. What I think you'll find is that Janet's perspective and approach will empower you to discover that mindfulness is completely achievable – not just theoretically but truly for *you*. As a result, I predict you'll finish this book with a feeling of confidence that you (yes, you!) can do this.

Mindful Awareness and Strategy: A Basic Mindfulness Toolkit has something to offer no matter what your relationship is to mindfulness practice:

- Newcomers will get a solid foundation in mindful awareness and a great launching pad to start their practice.
- Current practitioners will get a new way to think about and enhance their practice no matter what techniques they are using.
- Helping professionals and mindfulness teachers will get a strategic framework from which they can choose relevant and field-tested techniques to offer to those with whom they work, as well as clear instruction on how to guide these experiences "real-time" within the context of a typical client/student session.

Cultivating mindful awareness through your sensory experience, which is always available to you, can lead to profound and meaningful discoveries about yourself and the world around you. That is my wish for you and the promise of this book.

To your ever-expanding awareness and well-being,

Christine Trani
Senior facilitator, Basic Mindfulness Home Practice Program
whenmindfulnessmatters.com
whenconversationsmatter.com

Contents

Acknowledgements

My current teacher. First and foremost, would be to acknowledge and thank my teacher, Shinzen Young, and his training system, Basic Mindfulness. The inspiration of his work is a deep seed in me that continues to bear fruit and for that I am deeply grateful.

All my other teachers. I have been blessed to experience many excellent teachers, some directly, some through writing and digital media. I am grateful for the influences of Paramahansa Yogananda, John Laurence, Thich Nhat Hanh, Sister Annabelle Laity, Mark Sullivan, Ramana Maharshi, Nisargatta Maharaj, Adyashanti, Ajahn Sumedho, Jack Kornfield, Gil Fronsdal and Rodney Smith.

My editor. Bows to Karen Lawrence, my friend and editor who provided initial impetus (stern eye-to-eye look, words "do this *now!*") and followed with ongoing emotional support and keen editing expertise for the duration of the process. She was especially helpful in teaching me another way to write.

Readers. Deepest thanks to all of you who agreed to read various drafts of the manuscript and offered useful feedback, suggestions and comments: Emily Barrett, Larry Christenson, Debbie Hall, Georgia Jones, Alan Kaiser, Steve Lucia, Elizabeth Luthy, Todd Mertz, Meg Salter. Special thanks to Patricia Reilly for her excellent proofreading and Chris Trani for both reading the manuscript and writing the clear and thoughtful Foreward to the book.

Family and friends. Thanks to all of you who offered encouragement, support, humor, and wisdom of various sorts, from initial ideas to final product: Nora, my tolerant and wise daughter; Patricia and Steve, composed of part solid rock, part flexible sounding board; Alan, for insisting that a desk in his house *was* the best place for me to start writing; Elizabeth whose dharmic backbone held me up when necessary.

My clients and students. My deepest thanks and bows go to all my clients and students. You have been my greatest teachers. Through your participation, openness, vulnerability, patience, and courage you taught me more about using and offering mindfulness than I could ever have learned otherwise. May you all live with ease.

A Note to the Reader

As you read this text, please understand that complete credit is given to Shinzen Young for all of the original language, acronyms, exercise format, and many original ideas from Basic Mindfulness that he was generous enough to let me use, adapt for clients and students, and then express in this book. I have spoken to Shinzen, listened to his talks at retreats, and read nearly all of his writings over the past twelve years. It would have been impossible, without ruining the flow of this book, to quote him every time I used his words or rephrased an idea of his.

However, you should know that the sound and feel of Shinzen's creation, Basic Mindfulness, interpenetrates the book. Most notably his work is expressed in the fundamental Basic Mindfulness concepts and definitions (In/Out/Rest/Flow/Space, Concentration, Clarity, Equanimity); acronyms (ION); some teaching phrases he uses routinely ('have a complete experience', 'subtle is significant'); and my descriptions of being taught by him.

I have adopted the basics of his system of teaching and added new features of my own. These include my personal use and understanding of it, my years of psychological expertise, and clinical and teaching examples of strategic application of his system for my students and clients. I have taught parts of the 'toolkit' several times in Shinzen's Home Practice Program and frequently received the feedback–even from longtime students–that hearing my way of expressing his system helped people grasp it in new way. I understand this as similar to how

we can hear something new in a piece of music when it is played/
interpreted by a musician other than the composer.

Janet Sims
April 20, 2016

Introduction: A Black Bag Strategy

When I was growing up, a doctor's black bag sat in the closet near the front door of our house. It was packed and ready to grab at a moment's notice. My parents were physicians, and I remember them making both ordinary and emergency house calls, a common practice for doctors in small rural towns. To a child, the black bag was a source of endless fascination. It held funny-looking tools for exploring inside and outside the body, odd-shaped little bottles of liquids and pills, tongue blades, bandages, syringes, and more. It had a familiar, medicinal smell. I would pick up each object, explore it closely, then put it back in its place. When I felt bold, I would take one of the hard candies that I knew were a distraction or reward for some upset child.

As I grew older the question often occurred to me: "How did they know what to put in the bag?" The big words of the medical world my parents used seemed immense, hard to fathom. Out of that vast field, how did they decide what were the most useful tools to bring? What did doctors generally expect to see when they made house calls? What was the most beneficial thing they could offer to people?

What was their strategy for helping the most people with the fewest tools?

The image and memory of the black bag returned to me recently in my work as a clinical psychologist who uses mindfulness as a foundational component of psychotherapy. People ask me why I practice mindfulness-based psychotherapy and what is it that mindfulness brings. The short answer is that psychotherapy is about change, and awareness is fundamental to insight and transformation. It is difficult or impossible to alter something that is not in our awareness. Mindfulness trains awareness and yields insight, making it a perfect companion to psychotherapy.

There are many ways to train mindfulness (1,2,3). The system I use was developed by my teacher, Shinzen Young. His training program is known as Basic Mindfulness (BM). It was developed strategically, i.e. with the intention of combining the best that the Eastern contemplative traditions and Western science had to offer. I had been meditating using other systems for a number of years before stumbling upon Shinzen's *The Science of Enlightenment* (CDs, Sounds True). Shinzen became my teacher soon after that.

Sometimes Basic Mindfulness is described as "a science of sensory experience." The curriculum is a precise exploration of visual, auditory, and somatic sensory modalities (See, Hear, Feel). The emphasis on sensory experience makes Basic Mindfulness easy for most people to grasp intuitively. The program has techniques that originate from a variety of ancient traditions, but because everything we know comes through one or more of these senses in some way (e.g. a child's laugh is auditory information; the temperature outside is somatic information; seeing the dog and creating the mental image of "dog" is visual information), sensory awareness is emphasized. Basic Mindfulness is also being modified all the time based on Shinzen's work with students and his own insights. Studying with Shinzen is not unlike life in general: to be his student you have to be flexible and go with the flow of his creativity.

All Basic Mindfulness exercises offer strategies for:
- managing daily challenges
- increasing daily satisfaction
- boosting self-and-other-awareness (hence the term "insight meditation")
- changing behavior

The BM system references space and time frequently; thus, it is optimal for how we inhabit the sensory bodymind, which is located *now*, in a sensory world. With the intersection of neuroscience, attachment theory, trauma therapy, and mindfulness, psychotherapy practices have experienced a renewed focus on the integration of bodymind sensory awareness. *Mindfulness, mindful awareness,* and *sensory awareness* are used synonymously in this book and refer to the foundational skill of paying attention, a selective focusing of consciousness on an object that allows us to do everything else. Training awareness is like sharpening a tool or calibrating an instrument; when the tool of awareness has been sharpened and calibrated, it will serve us reliably in our everyday lives.

I was drawn to Basic Mindfulness for the following reasons:

- It begins with the strategy of making mindfulness modern and science-friendly.
- The goals and practices are clearly stated and reasons for their use explained.
- It uses precise definitions of how to practice.
- It offers strategic approaches to when and how to use mindfulness.
- Multiple exercises are offered (as opposed to maybe one or two).

In combination, these factors make BM interesting and versatile. They also make the system hard, even unapproachable, for many people. It is broad, deep, and complex, and in addition, it is changing all the time. Shinzen describes his dream of measuring what is happening in mindful awareness: "How much of what, when, and where, interacting in what ways, and changing at what rate." Not your typical description of contemplative training!

The writing of *Mindful Awareness and Strategy: A Basic Mindfulness Toolkit* (BMT) arose from the coalescing of three factors. The first was that I had been adapting a simpler version of the Basic Mindfulness exercises for use with clients and workshop students who wanted to learn a little bit of meditation, not an entire psycho-spiritual system. These same students and clients would often ask if a handout was available for them to take home.

Next was my participation in a professional group whose members were all exploring the use of mindfulness in their clinical work. No one had heard of Basic Mindfulness, so I discussed it as a system and gave examples of how I used it with clients. My colleagues probed me about exactly what I did as a therapist, about my personal mindfulness practice, and my clinical experience teaching it.

The final push came from Mary, a twenty-seven-year-old client who practiced faithfully for several months, and each week shared with me some story of how mindfulness had helped her. One day she asked me if I had a handout because she had taught her boyfriend how to relax, and then her mother asked to learn it too because she was so impressed with Mary's progress in handling her stress.

Telling people how I used the system personally, describing how I offered it to students and clients, and creating written materials, hand-outs, and workshops all forced me to look systematically at what I was doing. I discovered I had created my own "black bag": a few core exercises, key strategies both for facing challenges and turning away from challenges mindfully, building positivity. GREAT! The BMT focuses on strategic choice of exercises broadly useful for daily life situations. I use it personally, for public workshops, and as a foundation for my psychotherapy practice.

HOW TO USE THIS BOOK

My synthesis of meditation and psychological expertise may provoke questions about who can benefit from this book. The simple answer is: Anyone who wants to bring strategic mindful awareness to their daily lives. You may be a parent who wants to feel more present and calm in your relationship to your children. Or you are a student seeking to improve concentration for academic pursuits. You might wish to bring mindful awareness to the stresses of your work life. Maybe you'd like to be more present and skillful in your personal relationships. Perhaps you would like to learn how to take a break from "fixing" yourself and just appreciate things as they are.

The Basic Mindfulness Toolkit is a synthesis of psychological training and experience *plus* contemplative training and experience. Like a doctor's black bag, I believe the BMT has something for everyone wanting to learn and apply strategic mindful awareness.

My general advice for using the book is to first read through the techniques and case examples. Though I present an abbreviated version of Basic Mindfulness, there is still a lot of material to digest. As you do this, try a few exercises that appeal to you. Maybe there is a strategy that is right for your present needs or that was used in a case example to which you can relate.

If you can, hone in on one or two exercises you enjoy and/or that offer some immediate benefit. Practice those few exercises regularly, for about ten minutes most every day. Doing a few things (or even one exercise) regularly is more beneficial than trying to do everything available here. When people try to do too much, it is sometimes difficult to fit everything into their day, and they often quit. Making one technique "your own," that is, using it until you are confident with it and it gives you something, can last a lifetime. Regularity is more important than quantity or variety for developing an ongoing mindfulness practice.

Note that the BMT is not a replacement for learning more about the entire Basic Mindfulness System that Shinzen Young offers in retreats and in his Home Practice Program (Shinzen.org). The BMT is a simplified (but still powerful) subset of the BM techniques, including applications based on my own twenty-eight-plus years of mediation and thirty-plus years of clinical psychology practice.

Though the ideas for this book were developed in the course of my work as a psychologist, I have tried to use language and examples relevant to everyone, not only those seeking psychological help. It is my hope that anyone who wants to learn strategies of mindful awareness and create their own Basic Mindfulness Toolkit will be able to do so after reading this book.

The book has five parts:

1. The What and Why of Mindful Awareness
Part One outlines what mindful awareness is, why we practice it, and the goals we have in doing so. Included are explanations of mindfulness, practice goals, the primary technique of noting, and the turn toward/turn away focusing strategies, as well as two ways of relating to our own experience.

2. The How and Where of Mindful Awareness: The Contents of Your Toolkit
Part Two fills out the contents of the Toolkit, describing what sensory experiences combine (or compound) to make the psychological experiences commonly called Body, Mind, and World. We then learn exercises to make simple contact with the Body, Mind, and World

components, and more exercises to find rest and nurture positive states in them.

3. There's an App for That! Applications of the Basic Mindfulness Toolkit

Part Three offers general guidelines plus a step-by-step process for deciding what tool to use.

4. Case Examples Using The Basic Mindfulness Toolkit

Part Four presents numerous true-life examples of students and clients learning to use the BMT for their particular situations. It is organized around common challenges that we all experience, such as the stress of being a caregiver to someone with a chronic illness, or managing painful emotions such as anger, fear, or sadness.

5. Where Do I Go From Here?

Part Five offers some final advice for establishing a mindfulness practice routine; information on how to find practice groups and support from others; some guidance for posture; suggestions for using mindful awareness practice as a general health and maintenance tool; and finally, an FAQ section.

Part One
The What and Why of Mindful Awareness

Chapter One

What is Mindful Awareness?

In the introduction I mentioned that Basic Mindfulness (BM) is one of numerous systems for training mindful awareness. Mindful awareness is all about how and where we focus attention. According to the BM system, mindful awareness is defined as: "Three attentional skills working together: concentration power, sensory clarity, and equanimity"(1). These three skills are learned for the purpose of focusing attention on and processing sensory experience. What is sensory experience? Anything we *see, hear, and feel.* Sensory experience includes both *outer experiences* like sights and sounds and *inner experiences* like thoughts and emotions. Mindfulness refers to how someone is paying attention to a sensory event—with the skills of concentration, clarity, and equanimity.

To say that we are "practicing mindfulness" can mean we actually are practicing a technique to build the three skills. Or it can mean that we're using whatever level of competence we already have with those skills and expressing that degree of mindfulness in our daily lives. So practicing can be both the means to acquire a skill and the end the skill building produces.

CONCENTRATION

Concentration means being able to focus your attention on what *you* decide is relevant, rather than spacing out or being pulled here and there by distractions. Concentration also includes *how much* awareness you bring to the focusing. Like a solution of saltwater, which when highly concentrated has more salt per unit of liquid than a low concentration, when you are completely concentrated, one hundred percent of your awareness is locked onto the focus object.

We need concentration to do almost anything. Remember the last time you *lost* concentration when you were reading, or playing a musical instrument, or driving, or even listening to your partner? Concentration is a primary skill needed to do such things as learning a new skill like reading; addressing a situation that requires a novel solution, such as a puzzle or fixing a bike tire when you don't have the right tools; or integrating a procedure into practical use, such as using a new piece of software or a new game.

CLARITY

Sensory clarity defines one's ability to detect and keep track of which of the senses is active, even (perhaps especially) very subtle or vague sensations. Sometimes emotions arise and become intense quite rapidly. When baseline mindfulness is high, the earliest moments of these sensations may be detected so they don't "highjack" us (capture our attention) and push us into behaving in ways we regret. Sensory clarity also allows us to observe more characteristics of whatever it is we are perceiving, and to observe them in a broader and deeper way. One kind of clarity we develop is like the resolution power of a telescope or microscope: the blurriness of things far away or tiny goes away as the lens brings them close enough to see distinct stars or bacteria. So we might be able to distinguish what part of anxiety is a purely physical event and what part is an emotional event.

Another flavor of clarity that mindful awareness develops is the ability to detect sensations that are more and more subtle. Some examples are the earliest bit of tension in the body that signals we are afraid or angry, or the subtle sound of mental talk that is a fairly constant activity in the brain but operates just below conscious awareness when we are not paying attention to it.

EQUANIMITY

Equanimity refers to being in contact with what is active but not reacting one way or another. Sensations may be pleasant, unpleasant, or neutral, but there is no need to interfere with, add to, or change anything. How do you know you are being equanimous? With equanimity sensations may be intense, yet at the same time they don't seem to matter as much as they once did. Or sensations may be very positive, and simultaneously we feel free to let them go without reactivity. Here is an example of a client, a former athlete, who was typically very competitive. When watching sports, he usually had a strong desire for "his team" to win, so much so that he would fret about sporting events long after they ended. After learning about equanimity and practicing some exercises, he reported the following:

> *I was watching a football game with friends and getting sort of worked up about my team. I noticed this was happening and started to simply track restful sensations and also what was happening in my mind. Suddenly, things just seemed different. I was still aware I would be disappointed if my team lost, but even that was okay. I didn't feel "I must have this"; it could happen either way.*

This is an example of equanimity allowing either outcome, and the feelings associated with either outcome, without reactivity.

Using this skill-set of mindful awareness (concentration, clarity, and equanimity) over time can have multiple physical, emotional, and mental benefits (2). Often I am able to guide a student to a direct experience of one or more of these benefits the first time we meet. This could be an experience of deep rest, or the cessation of "rumination," such as repeating thoughts of a fight with someone, or of a sense of pleasure they had not noticed before. The experience may be brief, but the sense of relief is powerful and its impact can cement their interest in learning the skills. Here is an example of a first session with a client, Fran:

> *Fran reported ruminating thoughts, anxiety, and panic attacks that began in her teens; she is now a twenty-eight-year-old professional. After taking her history I asked her if she wanted to try an experiment in focusing for the few minutes remaining in the session. She agreed. I taught her the correct posture for sitting in a chair and then said, "I am going to describe some restful sensations to you. As I describe each one I want you to turn your attention to it, label it 'Feel Rest,' and concentrate intensely for a few seconds on the relaxed quality of that body part. Repeat the labeling process on that sensation until I guide you toward a new one."*
>
> *She did this for not quite ten minutes and then I rang the bell. Her response was this: "I have never been so relaxed in my life. What did you do? How did that happen? People always tell me, 'Just relax, just chill,' but before this no one ever really showed me how to do it. Can we do that again?"*

Clearly it was useful for Fran to learn how to contact rest and relaxation in her body, and she will be able to apply that skill to many other situations in her life. Over the years, clients who practice these techniques have come back saying they didn't know what they would do without them. The techniques are simple enough to memorize and do most anywhere, yet powerful in the impact they can have.

Chapter Two

Why Practice Mindful Awareness?

You might think at this point that though you understand that you're learning mindful awareness by developing these three skills (concentration, sensory clarity, and equanimity), you aren't sure how they can truly help you. To answer this, we need to look both at the *goals* in formal practice (sitting alone or in a group doing mindfulness exercises), and at *practical outcomes* that occur when we are being mindful in daily life.

PRACTICE GOALS

Complete Experience

"Have a complete experience," Shinzen said to me when I asked him exactly *what* I'm trying to do with this exercise. He was the first teacher who had answered me so simply and clearly. My initial response was one of immediate relief and I thought, "Oh, that sounds simple. I can do *that*." Then later, when I was practicing, I wondered exactly what he meant by having "a complete experience." My mind wanted an immediate answer and convinced me I knew what he meant the instant he said it. This is a typical example of the mind controlling things from a place of ignorance. Another question I should have asked is: "How does 'a complete experience' help me feel better and function better in my everyday life?"

On the surface, it makes obvious sense: We want to experience completely and fully what is going on at any given moment, not miss any of the details. We want to digest every morsel that is on our plate. Thich Nhat Hanh says that when you are not present to details of your life: "You have missed your appointment with life"(3). It would be like going to a movie but not watching or listening to what's happening on the screen. Later, if someone asked, "Did you go to that movie?" you could honestly reply, "Yes," but you did not really absorb or experience what the movie had to offer. It is the same with our everyday lives. Were you fully present for the events of this day, or did your attention get pulled into habitual thinking patterns of past memory or future planning, or spacing out? When we learn to have a complete experience, we are able to be fully present to our lives. We are thoroughly satisfied with the pleasurable bits and can experience the painful bits without suffering. Improving the quality of our presence with all experience is one major benefit of increased mindful awareness.

On a deeper level, however, the goal "have a complete experience" evolves depending upon the degree of precision in your equipment (that means you!). Think of a microscope or other measuring device; what you see or how accurate the measurement is relies on the exactness of the equipment. We may begin by having a complete experience of the surface of the Body|Mind|World. But as the skill of mindful awareness grows deeper, and then is combined with the influence of time, our experience is also deeper and more complete. What appears on the surface as Body|Mind|World begins to change at subtler levels. The material world looks very different when viewed with a regular versus an electron microscope. Gradually viewing all things with greater mindfulness reveals them to be not very thing-like at all. Rather, they are more energy/movement-like; more like constant activity/movement/change.

Flow

Flow refers to the deeper "movement, change, energy, or force present within a sensory experience" (4). It is the ever-changing aspect of all experience. Our thoughts, our emotions, our lives, the sun, the tree in our yard: everything is coming and going, getting bigger, getting smaller, and in constant flux. Life is, in fact, more fluid than fixed and rigid. One of the practice goals is to cooperate with this fact of nature and do what we can to notice, support, and join the flow of experience. Flow is both ordinary and also the force that allows life to be unique in every moment. It is "the regular, ordinary world viewed with radical fullness"(5).

It is easy to stay on the surface of life and never notice the flow that underlies all experience. If we stay on the upper boundary of our life we see it only as the separate and fixed (i.e. non-changing) events that it seems to be: people, trees, animals, houses, cars, countries. When life is seen only as disconnected, we fail to act in ways on the surface that also cooperate with the deeper organizing principles ever-present below.

Taste the Actions of the Core Skills

Each of the core skills—concentration, sensory clarity, and equanimity—offers something we might call the "active ingredient": that property or action that is responsible for the helpfulness of the skill. Each action has a unique "taste" or felt sensation that goes with it. As the action occurs we can sense if we are concentrated or clear or equanimous because we know that particular felt sense, the "taste" of each one. The more the action is present, the more we can taste it. Consciously tasting the action of the core skills reinforces them and makes us more able to produce them. It is a sort of loop, as in biofeedback. The more you feel/taste them, the more familiar you are with what it takes at conscious and unconscious levels to make them happen, and the more you *do* to make them happen (though you may not be able to say exactly how you do it). Let's look briefly at the active properties of each skill.

Concentration has several active properties:

- Concentrated focus allows attention to absorb and learn about the object of our focus, so concentration is at the foundation of learning anything we might glean about ourselves or the world. Concentration acts to enable insight. There is a taste or felt sense when we are absorbed into something.

- When we are concentrated on a particular experience, by definition we *are not* concentrated on other things available in awareness. So concentration acts by producing a **letting go** of everything else in order to focus for a while on one thing. Subtly at first we learn the taste of the action that is "letting go" at the same time we are learning to be absorbed in what is in awareness.

- Concentration produces calm in the mind and relaxation in the body. These qualities are very useful for renewing mind and body, undoing stress, and also for supporting physical systems such as the parasympathetic nervous system and immune system function. We can get a taste of our body and our mind renewing themselves by virtue of the tranquility born of concentration.

Sensory clarity provides the action of disentangling the various threads of experience, allowing us to see what is really happening rather than perceiving a surface illusion of what appears to be happening. When several sensory experiences are combined (e.g. mental image, mental talk, emotions in the body), they multiply and create the illusion of a much bigger experience that is commonly called flooding. Sensory clarity stops this cross-multiplying and enables us to manage limited individual sensory components. Another way to understand sensory clarity is as resolution power, such as what a microscope provides. A microscope magnifies pond water so that we are able to distinguish one organism or plant (visual experiences) from another, rather than the whole field being a blur of cloudy water. When sensations cross-multiply, our experience of them and response to them can easily be clouded. When experience is clear, we can taste that as being so very different from a cloudy or fuzzy experience.

Equanimity provides an action that is like the opposite of resistance. When we resist experience, it means that the natural flow of experience is interrupted. We interrupt by pushing experiences away or grasping them. Equanimity allows us to notice everything without interfering with it. Think of this as the way light reveals everything it shines upon but does not prefer one object over another. For me, the taste of equanimity is "lightness," as though I have been freed from something, freed from wanting things to turn out a certain way. Another way to put it is that everything *right now* is completely acceptable. I am free from needing/wanting things to be other than exactly how they are right now, even if that includes pain or loss.

In summary, our practice goals to develop mindful awareness consist of having a complete experience, cooperating with the flow of experience, and developing familiarity with taste for the three core skills of concentration, clarity, and equanimity.

PRACTICAL OUTCOMES

What are some naturally occurring practical outcomes we might look for from mindfulness practice? Knowing what these are, we can observe their presence and see the direct impact of mindful awareness on our everyday life experience.

Managing daily challenges

Everyday life includes physical, emotional, and mental pain. This is simply a part of the human experience. The body and mind feel challenges from hunger, fatigue, illness, fear, anger, sadness, aging, conflict, confusion, and so forth. External conditions can also produce pain: jobs, relationships, satisfactions all come and go. When we have mindfulness, we are more able to live happily with these naturally occurring painful conditions. The pain may be unavoidable, but without reactivity and resistance it is much less. Mindfulness also reduces pain by breaking experience into smaller, more manageable pieces. Each smaller bit may hurt less, while the whole can produce psychological indigestion (overwhelm).

People who text with their cell phones sometimes use the acronym "OMG," which stands for "Oh my God!" and is used to convey the drama or emotional distress of an event. Mindfulness helps take the OMG out of our experience. Think of a time when you let go of your mind's story about some physical or emotional pain and felt only your body's sensations without the mind reacting to them. We feel less pain when we are clear and not entangled in the mental story or emotional reaction *about* the pain.

Increasing daily satisfaction

Everyday life also includes a great deal of physical, emotional, and mental pleasure. Just think of all the wonderful sights, smells, tastes, pleasant relationships, and satisfying physical actions you experience every day! The very same mindfulness skills that help us manage pain actually make life's enjoyable situations even more so. Small pleasures seem to be larger because our attention is concentrated and we are consciously present to each experience. Whether we are making love, playing a musical instrument, savoring a meal, or simply watching the evening stars come out, if we are focused and concentrated only on the sensation at hand without the story in the mind, we notice clearly and deeply all the pleasures around and within us. And through the integration of equanimity and flow, there is less clinging to things, hoping they will continue after their time has passed.

Boosting self and world awareness

Mindfulness meditation is also known as insight meditation because this practice leads to increased insight into self and world. This makes sense, in a way, as the techniques have us focus specific attention on ourselves in particular ways. Paying a lot of attention to any feature of the world—listening to a symphony, seeing a friend's face, chopping an onion—increases our knowledge about that feature and helps us relate to it more skillfully. Though many of you have a purely secular interest in learning mindfulness, it is important to remember that these skills developed from Buddhism and other spiritual traditions. Mindful awareness skills fall on a psycho-spiritual continuum; they offer both psychological and, if desired, spiritual development. Psychologically they help us develop and function as human personalities, a key reason there is currently so much interest in using mindfulness in combination with human endeavors such as medicine, education, leadership, and so forth. Insights naturally arise when we apply concentration, clarity, and equanimity to the self and the world.

As part of a contemplative practice, mindful awareness skills gradually lead us to contact our spiritual essence (known by many names—Spirit, God, Source—and sometimes called Self). Contemplative practice is an end in and of itself. Before we contact our spiritual essence or Self, there is (usually) a long period of contact with and development of the human personality, or "small self." These contacts with the small self provide the insights that help us in daily living and also refine the personality. By "refinement" we mean something similar to the process by which gold is refined by separating it from the non-gold ore in which it is found. It is more of a take-away process than one of addition.

With mindfulness practice, the parts of the human personality that are not Self (or Spirit, or Source) such as unskillful thoughts or behaviors, greed, impulsiveness, and anger, begin to thin out, sometimes drop away. In modern Western society this use of mindful awareness is called therapeutic mindfulness. In Buddhism, personality insights are called "insight into self." Over time, and as the human personality matures we gain deeper insights about the self and world and things naturally change. Here is an example:

Ruth is a thirty-two-year-old unemployed artist and museum curator presenting with social anxiety and an eating disorder that began at age twelve. She came to me for help with her anxiety over getting back into the job market and was interested in using a mindfulness-based approach. Her history revealed that her exercise regimen took up several hours each day and, along with eating restrictions, left her weak and without energy most of the time. Although she reported prior treatment for the eating disorder she said she only wanted to work on the anxiety at this time.

As she requested, I ignored the eating disorder and worked with her on her career goals and social anxiety. I taught her mindfulness focused mostly on sensations in the body and reactions in the mind as she approached social and professional situations. After a few months we had this conversation:

Ruth: I want to talk about something, but I'm hesitant to bring it up, afraid of what you will say.....No, I know that I'm really just afraid of my own reaction.

Janet: Ok, why don't we do a meditation and simply notice what is present for you now in the Body–both emotions and physical sensations–as you consider talking about this important topic. (We do the exercise for ten minute.)

Ruth: I need to talk about this (about ninety seconds of silence)...I know what I want to do, I know how to do what I want to do, but one of the things that stands in my way from doing anything at all is ....well....you know, the whole food thing.

Janet: You mean the whole time-consuming food, body image, exercise thing?

Ruth: Yes, I'm just so tired and worn out. To do the things I want to do I need energy. Plus it takes so much time to maintain the workout schedule, but I know I'm also just afraid to change, to give all that up. What if I fail at work? At least I have this to rely on and feel like I'm okay.

Janet: It seems that you find yourself needing to choose between going after what you love, what you have passion for, and what is familiar and appears secure. Actually, I would suggest that you have only the illusion of security with an eating disorder.

Ruth: I "know" it's an illusion, but it "feels" so safe. But if I stay here, I'll just keep being stuck like I have been for years.

Subsequently we rarely spoke of her eating/exercise concerns in therapy. Gradually, however, Ruth changed her eating and exercise patterns enough to be able to do the work she wanted so much to do. She began enjoying her creative life again and started to volunteer at a museum. Ruth said that simply noticing regularly and deeply, without judgment, what she really desired and comparing that with what she was choosing that stood in the way of her desired goals made things clear. And the clarity made it obvious what she needed to do, as well as giving her motivation to risk making changes.

Changing behaviors

Behaviors are generated by thoughts in the mind and physical and emotional sensations in the body. It is very difficult to change something you cannot see/feel and understand. Mindful awareness teaches us to contact and clarify the sensations that make up body, mind, and world. With practice and time, we acquire insight into the interactions between body, mind, and world that drive our behavior. When we see things clearly and understand their interaction, our behavior often changes naturally.

Here is an example of how mindful awareness resulted in a simple but significant behavior change:

Matt is in his late 50s, a retired learning specialist who has trouble with self-care. He came for treatment to learn how to better manage his anxiety. He became quite skillful at this, while also becoming aware of how he ignores himself and over-functions for others. Today he looks weary entering the session and shares how busy he has been recently managing the extended visit of his daughter and her family while continuing to care for his wife who has muscular dystrophy and dealing with his own painful health issues.

Janet: So Matt, from what you are telling me it sounds like you have really had your hands full: playing host to out-of-town kids and grandkids, monitoring your daughter bickering with her husband, your wife's ongoing health needs, and then your own hernia! Overall, how are you feeling and doing with all this?

Matt: (responding immediately) Well, I have been too busy to have much anxiety. So that's good news!

Janet: Yes, that is good news. I'm pleased there is not much anxiety, but I'm wondering about the other impacts of all this activity. You certainly have been working very steadily for three weeks. Let's take a minute and focus both your mind and body, do a sort of check-up to see what you notice. (Matt agrees to this and I lead him in a ten-minute meditation, broadly exploring sensations in the body and thoughts in the mind.)

Matt: (Opens his eyes and sort of stares. It is evident that he has become a bit teary.)

Janet: What did you notice going on as you explored the body and mind more deeply?

Matt: Well, at first I was aware of lots of aches and pains in the body. Then the mind sort of created images of lifting kids, cooking, cleaning up after kids and everyone, the endless "to-do list" from my wife. I'm just sooo tired and didn't really realize it. I'm too old for all this! I have to stop doing so much for everyone else and take care of myself some of the time, even if it disappoints them.

Janet: *That sounds like just the right response to the infor-mation that came from listening to the entire bodymind. Though there may be a lot more to do, it is punishing to you to expect yourself to be the one doing it all. It's easy to ignore the "Warning: I need help!" signals your bodymind sends when you are so focused on the needs of others.*

Matt*: This time feels different, though. I know that I do too much for others, but this time I really noticed how things feel to me!*

Janet*: Yes, you made contact with how it feels to be you and had compassion for your present overworked state. That is true self-compassion.*

After this there was a noticeable shift in Matt toward being more attuned to his own needs, saying "no" to family and others making demands he could not meet.

Review of Part One

Now let's review the "whats" and "whys" of mindful awareness.

1. We have defined mindfulness as a skill-set consisting of concentration, sensory clarity, and equanimity.
2. We also learned that our practice goals are:
   - to have a complete experience
   - to recognize and cooperate with the flow of all experience
   - to learn to "taste" the actions of concentration, clarity, and equanimity
3. Finally, we have seen that with practice, some practical outcomes we may experience are:
   - managing daily challenges
   - increasing daily satisfactions
   - boosting self-and-other awareness
   - changing behaviors

In the next part, we move on to the "how" and "where" of mindful awareness, which become the contents of your Basic Mindfulness Toolkit.

Part Two

The How and Where of Mindful Awareness–
The Contents of Your Toolkit

We have just described the "what and why" of mindful awareness. Now the question is *how and where* we focus attention to train mindful awareness. The quick answer to *where* is: on ourselves! Using various ordinary sensations—everything we see, hear, and feel; sights, sounds, thoughts, feelings, body sensations—we focus our attention in a way that will develop the three fundamental skills. This section will help you put the focusing skills and the objects of focus together to create the actual tools of your BMT.

Chapter Three

Sensory Focusing Skills

Every day we have experiences that prompt us to understand ourselves or change some behavior, but we frequently don't know where to start. Hey, a "person" is a complex entity! A lot is going on and we can't see it all at once. I like to tell people: Basic Mindfulness is sensational!, meaning our effort to understand starts with sensations. Touching, feeling, hearing, and seeing: we *are*, and life *is* what our senses experience at each moment. Sensation is how we know we are alive; as humans, all our awareness is grounded in our sensory experience. Sensation is also what we seek out every day of our lives. Everything we know, experience, learn, or desire comes through our senses. By focusing systematically on sensations, we train our attention and learn about ourselves and our world.

NOTING

Noting is the *how* of training mindful awareness. Most (but not all) of the exercises in your toolkit will use *Noting*, which is basically noticing and labeling sensations as they arise. Mindfulness systems that use noting all have their own methods and categories of sensations. Here is the basic

> *Noting*
> A period of noting practice typically consists of a rhythmic sequence of acts of noting.

Noting is a two-part process in which the following take place:

- Acknowledge: You clearly acknowledge the presence of a sensory event.
- Penetrate: You focus intently for a few seconds on that sensory event.

During acknowledgment of sensation you have the option (but not the requirement) of labeling the event you have acknowledged. To *label* means to think or say a word or phrase that describes the event you are noting. While doing this, ignore distractions, i.e. let them arise, but in the background.

Labeling is a way of focusing attention on the sensory event you are noting, thus assisting concentration. There are standard labels for each sensation to reinforce sensory clarity. For example, the noting label "Hear Out" is used for ordinary sounds in the environment. "Hear" refers to anything auditory (hearing) and "Out" refers to events arising outwardly. For a taste of the noting technique, try this sound meditation for about ten minutes.

Meditation: Focus on Sound

- Begin to focus your attention on external sounds, either those occurring naturally or ones you choose to play through a headset or speakers. If for a moment there are no sounds, focus on silence as a restful state.
- When you hear a sound, mentally label it "Hear Out" and hold your awareness on the sound intently for a few seconds. If all or part of the sound should drop away, label that "Gone." If the sound is continuous, simply keep labeling every few seconds until it vanishes ("Gone") or your attention is drawn to a new sound.

Comments about Noting

Noting sensations with labels moment-to-moment helps us develop mindful awareness. The point is to notice clearly and completely what is happening; however, when you first start to use labeling, it may feel cumbersome, awkward, like you have to concentrate so much on the label that it isn't helping. *I can guarantee you that this is a phase and will pass.* It may seem difficult or even a waste of time at first, but you are learning a new way to experience sensations that over time will result in greater mindfulness.

It is okay to speak labels out loud, especially if you're having trouble concentrating or feel overwhelmed. It is okay to miss or skip labeling some sensations, in particular when they're coming so quickly that you simply cannot physically label fast enough. When they are coming too quickly, it is okay to aggregate and label. An example of this would be when you are noting and labeling mental images with your eyes closed and, like a movie, they are moving very quickly. It is also fine to guess if you are not sure you actually experienced a sensation. Sensations can be very subtle, so guessing is fine.

Most often students use mental labels, but ultimately labeling is optional. Once you learn how to label it is also okay to simply note (i.e. notice) without labeling, as long as you are clear about exactly what you are noticing. It is also the case that noting alone may help directly with reducing emotional reactivity (1). It seems to be the case that simply putting negative feelings into words (researchers used negative emotional images) calms the part of the brain associated with painful arousal by simultaneously increasing activity in the frontal cortex, our "executive" brain.

THE PRIMARY FOCUS OBJECTS

Sensations can arise both inwardly (e.g. mental images) and outwardly (e.g. external sights). Sensations arise as either physical body experience or emotional body experience, mental images and mental talk, external sights and sounds. I find that people most easily understand all of these different kinds of sensory events as belonging to one of three categories: body, mind, or world. Here is a chart of the sensations that go with Body|Mind|World:

Body | Mind | World Sensations

When you are focusing on...	You are experiencing...
Body	Emotional body sensations and/or Physical body sensations
Mind	Mental images and/or Mental talk
World	External sights and/or External sounds

With both students and clients I start using sensory description language in the first interview. Though the context for students and clients is different, they both invariably start by telling me a complex story about themselves and their situation and why they have come to see me. I find it helps to start breaking the complexities down into the more manageable categories of Body, Mind, and World. Here is an example from a conversation with a new client, Martha, as she talks about a budding relationship:

Martha: I've known this guy as a friend for a long time and then we started texting about something and then he asked me to hang out. I really liked being with him, but memories of my old boyfriend [who was manipulative and abusive] kept holding me back. And when I went home, I was confused about whether I really wanted to see this guy again. (becoming teary)

*Janet: Tell me, do you notice anything in your **body** right now as you are talking about this situation?*

Martha: (Eyes defocus as she looks inward) Yes, I keep thinking of the things my old boyfriend used to say and there is like a tightness in my chest.

*Janet: So, Martha, it seems two kinds of things are going on. One is in your **body**, that physical sensation of tightness, and the other is in your **mind**, the thoughts of the old relationship. Can you tell me, are the thoughts more in the form of mental talk about him, mental images of him, or both? The **mind** can think in both of those ways.*

Martha: Both, I think. I remember him saying things and sort of see him in my mind's eye at the same time.

*Janet: Very good! That kind of detail, knowing the different parts of your experience, will really help us learn to manage them. Now, check again in your **body**. Sometimes the **body** has physical sensations, like that tension you mentioned, and sometimes it has emotional sensations, like fear or sadness or joy or anger. Did you have any emotional sensations just now when you spoke of that situation?*

Martha: *Yes, I did. I was feeling something...mostly it was like anxiety, but I'm not exactly sure.*

Janet: *That's fine. Emotions can be strong or quite subtle. Subtle ones can be hard to detect and distinguish from one another. As we go along I'll teach you some exercises to help you learn to be clearer and clearer on just which sensations are happening in your **body** and in your **mind**. Now, would you be willing to try an experiment with me?*

Martha: *Sure, if I can do it.*

Janet: *This is very easy. You'll have no trouble. I'd like you to focus attention on that mosaic ball up there on the shelf. See if you can hold your attention on just the blue tiles in the mosaic, maybe even count how many there are.... (Teariness has stopped, and Martha's facial expression is one of intense concentration. After a few minutes I speak again.) Now you can stop the counting. Can you tell me what, if anything, you noticed as I asked you to focus on the ball there in the **world** outside of your body and mind?*

Martha: *Well, at first it was hard to shift my attention, you know, away from my feelings, but then I got interested in the ball. There are so many colors and it was a bit of a challenge to keep count of the blue tiles from here, so I sort of got lost in the task. Things felt calmer inside.*

Janet: *You did it perfectly, Martha. You might think I was just trying to distract you, but this was not absent-minded distraction. By purposely turning attention to the outer **world** you made the inner sensations of **mind** and **emotion** fade to the background. Now, I want to return to* *your concerns about the present situation, but we will refer to this exercise and these categories of **body, mind,** and **world** again, alright?*

You probably noticed that I taught Martha about the body, mind, and world (B|M|W) categories by using her own experience. As she narrated particular aspects of her experience I gave them names and offered a way to think about them that will help her detect those sensations. You might try this right now with some experience you have had recently. What part of your experience is in your body? What part of your experience is in your mind? What part of your experience is in the external world? Some of these may be harder than others to locate, but it is helpful to begin thinking about your experience in this way. I also find it helpful to use this handout that describes the B|M|W sensory categories and their noting labels:

B | M | W Sensations and Labels

When you are focusing on....	You are experiencing...	And the labels for this experience are...
Body	Emotional body sensations and/or Physical body sensations	**Feel In** (emotional-type body sensations) **Feel Out** (physical-type body sensations
Mind	Mental images and/or Mental talk	**See In** (mental images) **Hear In** (mental talk)
World	External sights and/or External sounds	**See Out** (external sights) **Hear Out** (external sounds)

All the exercises Martha will learn later will use some variation of the B|M|W categories. In the third column of the chart you see the terms "In" or "Out" depending upon *where* the sensation seems to arise (inner versus outer). In addition to inner versus outer characteristics, the sense experiences we track always present as visual (seeing), auditory (hearing), or somatic (relating to body. This chart clarifies the definitions of the noting labels (2):

Noting Labels and Definitions

Name	Definition
See	Any visual experience
Hear	Any auditory experience
Feel	Any somatic experience
In	Arising inwardly
Out	Arising outwardly

So, for example, the label "See In" refers to the mental images we see in memories, planning, and fantasy. The labeling process is optional and designed to support the noticing process, which is not optional. Sometimes people want to shorten the labels to just "See" or "Hear" or "Feel", which is perfectly acceptable as long as you are very clear with yourself about where you are focusing. All "Feel" sensations happen in the body, but "See" and "Hear" can be inward or outward. Sometimes people prefer creating their own labels. Again, as long as you are clear about what and where your focus is, this can work fine. The point is to notice with concentration, clarity, and equanimity. However, there are reasons for the labels being what they are and at the beginning I encourage students to use the standard labels first.

Six Focus Exercises

In this section you will learn six focus exercises that are excellent for stand-alone mindful awareness training but can also be combined in various ways to fit different life situations that may arise.

The first three exercises teach us to make simple contact with the three primary focus objects we have just discussed in detail: Body|Mind|World. *All ordinary human experience is visual, auditory, or somatic and going to be in one or more of these three locations.* When we can mindfully detect what is going on there, i.e. with concentration, clarity, and equanimity, we have a very solid starting point for adapting to whatever circumstances we encounter.

Exercise One – Focus on Body

In my experience, it is easiest and most intuitive to start by focusing on the somatic aspect of experience. We do this by paying simple, direct attention to various kinds of activity in the body. Most people coming to therapy are surprised to find that they are significantly out of touch with sensations in the body. Focusing skillfully on somatic sensations has many benefits, such as:

- Making us familiar with body signals of comfort and discomfort
- Helping us detect the physical and emotional components of any experience; by subdividing the whole body into smaller parts, we make this more manageable
- Improving function in movement, balance, posture, and generally inhabiting the body more fully

- Enabling us to interrupt the ruminating mind at will
- Allowing us to have a more complete experience of whatever is happening, leading to greater insight and less residual or "unfinished business" lodged in the body as muscle tension

Another important feature of the body is that some of its experiences (sensations) arise inwardly and some of them seem to come from the external world. It really inhabits both realms and so contributes to the sense of there being a "me" located "here" and the "world" located "there," when in fact we are one interconnected whole. We use the sense of touch to make things in the so-called external world part of us, as when we use tools or drive a car. Food is literally transformed by our digestive system to *become* the body.

We frequently feel overwhelmed by too much going on in the body physically and/or emotionally. By making simple contact and tracking physical experiences one at a time, moment to moment, we learn to deconstruct body into its component parts (we will also learn to do this with mind). This trains our ability to face and experience sensations with equanimity rather than fight with them or disconnect and turn away from them. Two now well-known equations go like this:

Suffering = Pain x Resistance (When we resist pain, it becomes suffering; the more resistance, the more the suffering.)

Empowerment = Pain x Mindful Awareness (When we turn toward pain, we feel empowered to have our experience and the wisdom inherent in each sensation; the more mindful awareness, the more empowerment.)

It is important for *everyone* (beginning or advanced) to be able to track what is going on in the body. This kind of focus at the beginning lays a foundation for a path of meditation, self-care, and ultimately more advanced psycho-spiritual work. It is essential for having a complete, ordinary human experience. Here is an exercise focusing on the sensory events of the body:

Exercise: Focus on the Body

The purpose of this exercise is to broadly explore physical and emotional sensations in the body. Sensations could be active or restful, stable or flowing. The sensation of something you observe vanishing is also included.

Body or somatic activity can be experienced in two ways: emotional-type body sensations and physical-type body sensations.

- Emotional-type body sensations may include anger, fear, sadness, embarrassment, impatience, disgust, interest, love, joy, gratitude, smile, laugh, and so forth. These sensations may be strong, mild, or non-existent in the body. If they are non-existent, enjoy that as a restful emotional state. Peace is also a restful physical sensation. The full label for any emotional-type body sensation is "Feel In." You may also choose the single word label "Feel."
- Physical-type body sensations may include hot/cold, muscle contraction, pain, non-emotional breathing, non-emotional pulse, hunger, thirst, itching, aching, muscle tension, gas or bladder sensations, contact with clothes, air, and so forth. When there is relaxation in the body, enjoy that as a restful physical sensation. The label for any physical-type body sensation is "Feel Out." You may also choose the single word label "Feel."

Instructions

Whenever you notice an emotional-type body sensation, note "Feel In." Whenever you notice a physical-type body sensation, note "Feel Out." If you prefer to use the single word "Feel," just be clear what sensation, physical or emotional, you are noticing. If both should occur, just note one; it doesn't matter which one. If something you are noting should diminish or drop away completely, note "Gone." If nothing much is detectable either physically or emotionally, note that as "Feel Rest" or "Feel" and hold awareness on the peace or relaxation present in the body.

Practice this exercise for at least ten minutes.

Exercise Two – Focus on Mind

Now let's look at the experience we call "mind." Most of the time we're using the mind and don't stop to notice exactly what the mind itself is and how things work up there. First, let's clarify that for this book the term "mind" refers to our thinking process. It is a human function made up of auditory and visual sensations. These sensations create pictures and language that the mind uses to represent things, such as places, objects, and people in the external world as well as abstract "things" that don't exist except as ideas.

Many of my students and clients talk about being overwhelmed by their thoughts. Either the contents are painful or there is simply too much thinking activity. How often have you or someone you know said, "If I could just figure this out I —"? My take is that we get paralyzed precisely because the repeated attempt to "figure it out" is a mental act and only adds more ineffective sensation to an already overloaded mental system.

When I invite people to stop using their analytical mind to "figure things out" and instead start tracking simpler sensations such as mental images or physical body sensations, moment to moment, their overwhelm recedes. Why? There are at least three reasons:

- The problem is not solvable by the reasoning mind, so to use "thinking" is like using a hammer on sore muscles when you really need a massage or warm bath.
- When we stop using an action that isn't working, we feel relief.
- When there is too much sensation without clarity and equanimity, the intensity of the sensations cross-multiply to create the somatic/cognitive illusion of more intensity than is actually present. The result is overwhelm in the whole body-mind-world system.

As we did with the "Focus on Body" exercise, we will again use the noting technique to track the mental or mind aspect of our experience. The name of this exercise is "Focus on Mind." In it we will focus on the two sensations that make up the thinking process: mental images and mental talk.

Exercise: Focus on the Mind

The purpose of this exercise is to allow attention to broadly float between the sensory experiences that make up the mind or thinking process. The mind can be active or restful, and sensations that diminish or drop away completely can also occur frequently.

Mind or thought activity can be experienced in two ways:

- *Visually*, as mental images, anything that is visual and arising inwardly. Mental images are usually of people, places, or objects. They can be vivid but are more often fleeting, vague, or ghostlike. If images are not present (mind is blank) then the darkness/brightness of the blank can be seen as a form of visual rest. The label for any visual mind sensation is "See In." You may also choose the single word label "See."
- *Auditorily*, as mental talk, anything that is auditory and arising inwardly. If mental talk occurs, listen to it with detachment, neither suppressing it nor identifying with it. If nothing auditory is arising (quiet), listen to this as a form of auditory rest. The label for auditory mind sensation is "Hear In." You may also choose the single word label "Hear."

Instructions

Whenever you notice a mental image or blank, note "See In." Whenever you notice mental talk or quiet, note "Hear In." If both occur, just note one; it doesn't matter which one. If you prefer, you may use the single word labels of "See" or "Hear," but be clear that you are focusing on inner sensations and ignore external sights and sounds. If something you are noting diminishes or drops away completely, note "Gone."

Practice this exercise for at least ten minutes.

Now we have exercises to deeply explore both body and mind. Body and mind sensations together make up what most of us experience as the "self," or as I sometimes call it, the "self-sense." The self-sense is the "I" or "me" or "my" we are referring to whenever we express preferences like "I want" or "I don't want" or "my feelings." For this reason, having specific skills for noticing what is happening in body and mind is useful when we are pained, unhappy, or interested in changing behaviors.

Exercise Three – Focus on World

Combined, the physical sights and sounds around us make the world that we live in. Unlike contents of the mind that can be in the past or future, these events occur in the "now," allowing us to become anchored or grounded in the present moment. This anchoring may become so intense, especially with sounds, that we can feel merged with the sensation, with no boundary to distinguish "I" (listener) and "It" (the sight or sound).

Our "world" can include anything that we see and hear. It encompasses the range of the most ordinary to the most extraordinary sights and sounds. The slap of your feet walking, the whoosh as the cars go by on the street, the chirping of a bird, the roar of an airplane, the beauty of a flower, the arguing voices as you pass a couple on the sidewalk, the smile on your partner's face when she comes to greet you, the squeak of the swing on the playground and the child in the swing, the stern faces around the table at the board meeting. These are but a few examples of the external world we live in.

Physical touch can be so connected to the world that people ask, "Why don't you include the physical touch of objects in your category of world?" As previously noted, physical touch is a unique sensation because it spans the spectrum of what people experience as "me versus not-me." The skin barrier creates the experience of certain physical sensations arising "in here," while others seem to arise "out there." Sometimes touching an object can feel like "me or mine"; the object becomes an extension of our own body, like using a fork to eat. And sometimes touching an object feels like "not me," such as eating with a non-familiar implement such as chopsticks. For simplicity, in the Basic Mindfulness Toolkit all somatic sensations are part of body, even those that seem at times to be more world (or "not-me"). Keep in mind, however, that boundaries are flexible, and the sense of identity (I, me, mine) may expand to include all that makes up the so-called "outer world" such as clothes, car, spouse, etc.

Another observation people often make is that the focus on world seems like a distraction from distressing thoughts and feelings, or simply avoidance. Though it is similar to distraction, there is a subtle but important difference. We are systematically practicing "See Out" and "Hear Out" to develop the ongoing mindful awareness skills of concentration, clarity, and equanimity. While we may exploit the ability of this focus to temporarily give relief from inner discomfort, overall it is part of strategically building skills that produce mindful awareness.

Now let's practice focusing on the world.

Exercise: Focus on the World

The purpose of this exercise is to use the natural attraction power of external sights and sounds to help you stay anchored in the here and now. To facilitate that, it's okay to intentionally look at pleasant objects or scenes you enjoy; for example, note "See Out" while walking in nature. Likewise, listening to music you enjoy can be an excellent "Hear Out" focus as long as you stay with the auditory experience and do not get lost in thoughts and images triggered by the music. If you prefer, you may also use the one-word labels "See" and "Hear" as long as you are clearly focused on external sights and sounds. Ignore any internal talk or images.

Allow attention to broadly float between the elements that make up the compound experience of the outer world. With your eyes open, focus continuously on external sights and/or sounds, leaving interior thoughts and feelings in the background of awareness. Your attention may be drawn to some visual object or it may be drawn to particular sounds. Just pick one of these to focus on. Visually, note each time your attention shifts from one object to another or from one place in an object to a different place in that object.

Sounds may be discrete (as when a bird chirps or a car passes by and fades out) or more continuous (the hum of a refrigerator, music).

If your eyes get tired, intentionally de-focus your gaze for a moment and then return to noting sights, or shift to sounds. If you shift modalities from sight to sound (or vice-versa) and the first modality vanishes, note this as "Gone." It doesn't matter if you are drawn more to one or the other modality, but do note sensations in both modalities at some point in the exercise.

Instructions

With your eyes open, place some awareness in both the sights and sounds of your external environment. If you are drawn to sight, let your line of vision freely float from direction to direction, object to object, or place to place within an object.

If your awareness is drawn to sound, note "Hear Out" or "Hear." If all or part of the sound diminishes or drops off completely, note "Gone."

Each time your line of sight shifts, note "See Out" or "See." It does not matter if the shift is spontaneous or intentional. Nor does it matter if the shift is due to a physical movement of the eye or just a movement in attention. If all or part of the sight vanishes, note "Gone."

If you shift between sight and sound modalities and notice the preceding one drop away, note "Gone." If both arise at the same time, just pick one to notice.

Practice this exercise for at least ten minutes.

Review of First Three Exercises

Let's review the three exercises presented so far. Each uses the noting technique and specific labels to make contact with the sensory events that make up the experiences of body, mind, and world. The sensory events are all some form of visual, auditory, or somatic modality (seeing, hearing, feeling). They also can be seen as arising inwardly or outwardly, as subjective or objective experience. All of these ways of categorizing sensory experience can be useful at different times in various situations. The myriad options allow us to make meaningful contrasts that deepen our understanding.

For example, sometimes we want to notice the body as a whole and sometimes it's best to distinguish the emotional from the physical body. At times it can be helpful to limit experience to a particular modality, just to seeing or hearing of feeling. In other situations we want to know our experience from the standpoint of what is subjective (seems to be happening on the inside) and what is objective (seems to be happening on the outside). All of these distinctions and contrasts have practical utility and increase our insight into ourselves. Here is a graph that puts all of the sensory elements, their modalities, their definitions, their locations, and standard labels into one big picture:

Body | Mind | World

Modality, *Definition*, In/Out, **Label**

Sensory Modality	Inwardly Arising	Outwardly Arising
See	**See In** *Explore internal sight*	**See Out** *Explore external sight*
Hear	**Hear In** *Explore internal sound*	**Hear Out** *Explore external sound*
	Mind	**World**
Feel	**Feel In** *Explore emotional body sensations*	**Feel Out** *Explore physical body sensations*
	Body	

If you went no further than using these first three exercises to make concentrated, clear, and equanimous contact with the body, mind and world, you would have collected a very helpful set of skills that would certainly develop mindful awareness and could be applied to numerous challenging situations. Many traditions use a single sensation, the breath, for cultivating mindfulness. But the Basic Mindfulness Toolkit offers even more options and flexibility with the next three exercises that focus on the characteristics of "rest" (relaxation), "flow," and "positive," which can arise within any of the Body|Mind|World categories.

Exercise Four – Easy Rest: Relaxation and Grounding

So far, the exercises in our BMT have been directed primarily toward detecting *activity* in the body, mind, and world (although we did have the option to notice rest in the *Focus on Body* exercise). We do this to make simple contact and become familiar with active sensations in order to live and work with them effectively. However, relaxation is also a key feature of physical and psychological well-being. Likewise, relaxation is also one of the major benefits of mindfulness practice. Most meditation training systems have some form of emphasis on rest or tranquil states, so we want to include exercises for rest and relaxation in our toolkit.

We can understand rest as either the *presence of something*, such as relaxation or peace in the body, silence in the mind or world, and so on, or we can see it as the *absence of activity* in body, mind, and world. With Easy Rest, you are allowing attention to move back and forth between two soothing sensations that can be easily found or created. The sensations we move between are physical relaxation and the blankness we see with eyes closed. Whereas other forms of rest such as the absence of physical sound or the absence of mental talk in our heads may not be available, Easy Rest sensations are always available, hence the term "easy."

Finding and creating rest is important for many reasons (3). Let's look at a few of the physical and psychological ones:
- Our modern world produces stress for most everyone. Chronic stress puts the body in a constant state of high arousal, triggering stress hormones that arouse the sympathetic nervous system's

fight or flight mode. Physical relaxation (rest) is the default state we are *supposed* to be in most of the time and is associated with the parasympathetic nervous system: rest and digest. It happens that Easy Rest is my favorite "go to" exercise because I get quick relaxation in much of the body *and* mind. I use it so often that it has become a reliable tool for me to get quick but deep rest throughout my day.

- In the rest state there is low tension and absence of arousal for specific action so the body is free to devote resources to reproduction, digestion, cell and tissue repair, immune system building, etc. When we can enter restful states at will, we are helping our bodies do what they need to do to stay healthy.

- Finding and creating rest allows us to get away from sensory challenges while still developing the core skills of mindfulness—a sort of win-win practice. I believe this is the reason so many students and clients choose to do rest practices when I give them the choice of exercise.

- Restful states are pleasurable for almost everyone. They can produce a sense of contentment independent of external circumstances (such as being able to relax while waiting in a crowded airport). When we are able to find contentment any time we want, we feel independent and empowered.

- In addition to providing relief for body and mind, restful states also lead to a sense of being *grounded*: when awareness is tranquil and supported by its connection to the present moment, the body, and the solidity of the physical reality around us. My first Vipassana teacher, Thich Nhat Hanh, would focus on the calming and relaxing properties of the breath to teach students how to feel stable right away. Making contact with relaxation in the body is so important that some form of it is found in all the major traditions of meditation. It helps us stay anchored in the now (4).

Now let's practice the Easy Rest focusing technique:

Easy Rest Exercise

The purpose of this exercise is to randomly focus on mental rest and somatic rest. **Mental rest** comes from closing our eyes and letting go of visual activity: outer sights and inner images. This kind of exercise is known to create alpha waves in the brain, which represent a state that is both restful and alert.

Somatic rest includes physical and emotional components. Physical rest refers to settling in with a posture, relaxing muscles, and so forth. Emotional Rest refers to the *absence* of emotion in the body.

Visual Rest:

Eyes closed: Focus on the darkness, brightness, or the mixture of darkness and brightness you see in front of and/or behind your eyelids when you close your eyes. We'll refer to this form of visual rest as "grayscale blank." The standard label for this is "**See Rest**." You can also use the one-word label "See" as long as you're clear that you are focused inwardly on the grayscale blank.

When you are focused on the grayscale blank, patches of dark or bright may disappear. Such a disappearance is a well-defined example of "Gone."

Somatic Rest:

Focus on physical and emotional restful states in your body. The label for physical or emotional rest is "Feel Rest." You may also use the one-word label "Feel" and know that it refers to the feeling of relaxation or emotional peace in the body.

There are many ways of feeling Rest: Learn to *find* it:
- By focusing on how your muscles relax into a still posture
- By noticing how your core muscles (rib cage and diaphragm) automatically relax each time you breathe out
- By noticing when your body is *without* emotional feeling

Learn to *create* it:
- By stretching up and settling into your posture
- By intentionally relaxing individual body parts (face, jaw, shoulders, arms, and so forth)
- By breathing into emotional sensations to soothe them without, however, trying to beat them down! ("Breathing in" means focus on the location of the emotional sensation and visualize the breath going in and out of the emotion as you breathe. This is most often in the chest or gut area but could be an absence of tension in the face, arms, shoulders, or anywhere.)

Instructions

With eyes closed, tune into the restful aspect of visual and somatic experience. Allow your attention to broadly float between grayscale blank (the darkness/brightness in front of or behind your closed eyes) and the physical relaxation and emotional peace in the body. When you are aware of a mental blank, note "See Rest"; when you are aware of physical or emotional rest in the body, note "Feel Rest." If more than one arises, just pick either to focus on. If all or part of what you are noting drops away, note that moment "Gone."

Practice this exercise for at least ten minutes.

Exercise Five – Easy Flow: Change and Endings

In the first chapter we talked about contacting and cooperating with Flow as one of the practice goals. We understand that events in life at all levels are changing, coming, going, ending all the time. This means that nothing is truly fixed; everything is impermanent. When we begin to pay special attention to just the change and impermanent qualities of any sensory experience, we're getting in touch with the Flow that is fundamental to all experience.

Contacting Flow is actually another way to deconstruct body, mind, and world and thus feel less gripped by challenging sensations on the surface. Contacting Flow means to sense the fundamental movement and change forces *behind* what you see, hear, and feel. This is very useful in everyday life, because by looking through or beyond pain to the forces behind it, you begin to break the hold of painful sensations that control you. Instead of pain being the primary focus, it dissolves as the Flow qualities behind it come into focus.

One special case of Flow you have already practiced is noting "Gone" when the change is as something suddenly ceases. Much relief comes from the direct experience that all things, especially painful things, come to an end. There are many flavors of Flow (change) in the Basic Mindfulness System and "Gone" is a special case.

In addition to the vanishing of the "Gone," Flow can have different qualities: wavy and undulatory like seaweed, or vibratory and buzzing like electricity. It is also present whenever there is increase or decrease of intensity, size, or location, as when things get louder/softer; faster/slower; more painful/less painful, etc. Inward and outward pressure forces are also Flow. Flow is in us and all around us, but generally we encounter Flow in sights and sounds quite regularly: seeing and hearing the flutter of leaves; the sound of passing cars as the hum of tires rises, falls, then stops altogether. We also experience Flow internally as breathing, heart rate variability, and waves of emotion that move through our core or up our spine.

Despite the fact that Flow is happening in the body, mind, and world all the time, we are not always able to detect it. This next exercise is called *Easy Flow* because, like *Easy Rest*, these two flavors of Flow are always detectable for practice.

Easy Flow Exercise

The purpose of this exercise is to focus generally on breathing but more as a dynamic process (Flow, force, movement) than a physical sensation. We will alternate between two types of sense Flow—somatic and visual—that are present whenever we breathe. The physical sense Flow is labeled "Feel Flow" and the visual sense Flow is labeled "See Flow." Here are some examples:

Feel Flow
"Feel Flow"" in this exercise is the movement, energy, or change that comes with the physical or emotional sensations of breathing, such as:
- the feeling of increase or decrease as the chest and lungs expand to let air in and contract to release carbon dioxide
- inward and outward pressures when the in breath pushes the shoulders up slightly and the out breath allows them to drop slightly. Or a faint tickle of clothing rubbing against skin as the shoulders rise and fall, or the abdomen expands and contracts
- speeding up or slowing down the rate of breathing

- coolness in the nostrils as you breathe in, warmth as you breathe out
- changing emotions in the body, such as fear, sadness, contentment, joy, etc.
- any form of change, force, or movement you detect in your body as you breathe

See Flow

"See Flow" in this exercise refers to the spontaneous movements, energy, or changes in visual experiences that arise with our eyes closed as we attend to the body breathing, such as:
- mental images of the rising and falling of the chest or abdomen
- mental images of air coming into the nostrils or in and out of the lungs
- mental images of any subtle body movements associated with the breathing process, such as images of the chest, the shoulders, the nostrils, etc.
- swirling and vibrating in the "grayscale blank" behind your closed eyes
- any form of visual movement, energy, force, or change you see with eyes closed

Gone

Detecting "Gone" within Flow is easy while following the breath because it is obvious and regular. The in breath starts, reaches a peak, then stops—that is a "Gone." The out breath then starts and at some point comes to an end—another "Gone." We can be noting "Feel Flow" or "See Flow" when the "Gone" occurs; it doesn't matter which. In addition to any other vanishings we might detect, we can note "Gone" at the end of each in breath and out breath, or at the end of the entire in and out breath.

Instructions

With your eyes closed, center your attention on your breath. This could be at the chest or abdomen rising and falling, the nostrils as air passes in and out, or floating between all three locations. Allow attention to broadly float between "Feel Flow"and "See Flow". If you prefer to use the one-word labels "See" or "Feel" you may, but be clear that it is visual or somatic flow in those spaces you are labeling. If something you are noting drops away or vanishes entirely, note "Gone." Some of these sensations are quite subtle, so it's okay to guess. Remember, subtle is significant!

Practice this exercise for ten minutes.

Exercise Six: Nurturing a Positive Body|Mind|World: Self-Compassion and Reconstruction

Most of us spend a lot of time looking at the troubles in our lives. We focus on illnesses, accidents, body aches, emotional distress, the challenges of balancing career, relationship, and childrearing, financial stressors: the list goes on and on. We look for the problems and try to fix them in hopes we will feel and function better. Fortunately, our toolkit is gradually filling up with tools that can help us make clear contact with ordinary experience or effectively manage troublesome sensory experiences.

It's not enough to handle the negative experiences of life. Neuroscience and the field of Positive Psychology have shown that our minds preferentially search for and store unpleasant memories as a protection (5). Negative, instead of positive, emotional experiences get saved by the brain. You can imagine that over a lifetime this can add up to a negative self-concept, a risk for anxiety and depression, not to mention that our view of the world is totally skewed to the negative, what scientists call "negativity bias."

Fortunately, our brains can change! The process is called neuroplasticity: the ability of the brain to change itself when new neuronal pathways are engaged. When we have new experiences, new parts of the brain are activated. We can alter our brains by changing the way we think. It happens that mindfulness is one of the practices that promotes neuroplasticity.

To offset the "negativity bias" we have to regularly focus on the good stuff happening in body, mind, and world (6). But we can't do it just once. It's kind of like creating a new pathway in the woods. Walking down it one time won't make much difference, but the more often we use that path the easier it is to use. And in the brain, the pathway recruits other neurons to fire together, making the path wider and stronger the more it is used.

In Basic Mindfulness we do this by finding or creating pleasurable events and then savoring them in the body. Looking closely, we notice that subtle pleasant feelings such as gratitude, love, enjoyment of natural beauty or a bird in a tree are already happening; we simply have to notice them deeply. It is also possible to generate new, pleasant feelings such as self-compassion, kindness, joy, acceptance, and then savor these feelings in order to reinforce them.

Besides helping us feel better in the moment, the benefits of increasing positive emotions can be enduring. Researcher Barbara Fredrickson has reported the following benefits (7):
- a stronger immune system
- a cardiovascular system that is less reactive to stress

- a general lifting of mood
- increased optimism and resilience
- the ability to counteract the effects of painful experience

The BMT contains a simplified version of the Nurture Positive technique offering two exercises to reconstruct body and mind with positive content. The first one creates more general positive emotions such as gratitude, friendliness, kindness, joy, enthusiasm, and so forth. The second one is a set of affirmations to enhance the specific emotion of self-compassion in body and mind (8).

Nurture Positive does not use the primary noting technique. Both the generic and self-compassion Nurture Positive exercises follow the same two-step format:
- Select mental images and/or mental talk that support positive feelings for you. The images could be things that have actually happened: a pleasant vacation, the taste of a tangerine, the sight of your child's face, a successful work product, the plant on your windowsill. Or they may be things you would like to happen in the future such as a new job or quitting smoking. The word/image combinations can be simple (eating a tangerine) or more complex experiences (a pleasant vacation) but really can be anything you feel pleasure from. Hold the image/talk combinations in the mind.
- Notice any pleasant feelings that arise in the body, particularly emotional sensations, and hold attention on them intently (savor them) for 10-20 seconds or until they disappear.

Generic Examples of Nurture Positive image and word combinations:
- "tangerine" (with an image of eating it at lunch)
- "Alison" (with an image of your child sleeping)
- "table" (with an image of the table you finished sanding/polishing)
- "vacation" (with an image of the lake, beach, country, city, hike

you enjoyed)
- "orchid" (with an image of an orchid someone gave you)
- "gratitude" (with an image of something you feel grateful for)
- "friendly" (with an image of someone toward whom you want to feel friendly)

Self-compassion: Nurture Positive sentences (words only). Follow the same procedure, except use the following sentences for the mental talk, creating an image that corresponds to each statement. Notice the impact on the body for 20-30 seconds, then repeat and hold the sentence a second time before going on to the next. The first group of sentences is longer and more specific. The second group is from traditional loving kindness practices.

Long version (more detailed and specific)
May I be kind to myself
May I have compassion for myself
May I be free of suffering
May I be safe
May I be filled with physical health and vitality
May I have inner peace and contentment
May I have clarity and wisdom
May I live in love and harmony
May I accept myself
May I live with ease
May I be happy
May kindness and self-compassion grow daily

Short version (traditional loving kindness meditation)
May I be safe
May I be happy
May I be healthy
May I live with ease

Nurture Positive Exercise

The purpose of this exercise is to trigger pleasant sensations and sustain them in a way that allows them to be savored, letting them sink in as we would the warmth of bath to penetrate our body. It is not a problem if you have negative thoughts or feelings; just leave them in the background of awareness.

Instructions

Choose either a **generic** word/image combination or one of the **self-compassion** versions of Nurture Positive and:

Select mind activities (mental images and mental talk or affirmations) that support positive emotions.

Notice any pleasant sensations that arise, particularly pleasant emotions. Hold attention intently on the sensations for 10-20 seconds. Savor the positive sensations and leave any negative sensations in the background of your awareness. If no positive emotions are present, hold awareness on the mental images and mental talk for the 10-20 seconds.

Practice this exercise for ten minutes.

Review of Part Two

In Part Two we were introduced to the contents of the Basic Mindfulness Toolkit.

1. First, we learned that everything in ordinary awareness is a sensory event; thus, everything in awareness is some form of seeing, hearing, or feeling.
2. Next, we were introduced to a primary noting technique used for focusing on sensations.
3. Third, we learned which sensations to focus on using the noting technique; what sensations make up our experience; that there is the body, the mind, and the world.
4. Finally, we learned exercises for Rest, Flow, and Nurturing Positive in the body, mind, and world.

Part Three will offer many examples of how to use these focusing skills in everyday life, as well as methods for applying them to relieve discomfort, increase satisfaction, and improve behavior.

Part Three

There's an App for That! Applications of the
Basic Mindfulness Toolkit

Chapter Four

General Guidelines for Applying Mindfulness Exercises

The ability to pay attention is required to do most everything, which is why mindful awareness is so broadly used nowadays in medicine, psychotherapy, education, business, and other fields. This section will teach you how to *strategically* apply mindfulness to emotional and behavioral challenges that often bring people to see a therapist. But first, let's look at some guidelines that will be helpful for anyone using the Basic Mindfulness Toolkit.

USE THE BODY|MIND|WORLD CATEGORIES

The first and most basic guideline is to begin to think in terms of the body, mind, and world categories you have been taught to focus on with the noting technique. In other words, **no matter what experience you are having, it is happening in the body, the mind, and/ or the world, so ask yourself**: What part of my current experience is happening in the body (physical and emotional sensations)? What part of my current experience is happening in the mind (mental images, mental talk)? What part of my experience is happening in the outer world (sight and sound)?

This first strategy, assigning sensory experiences to these ordinary categories, will help you right from the start. The habit of seeing experience in these categories immediately improves clarity about what is happening both subjectively and objectively in your surroundings. It also gives you something effective to do when you are confused, overwhelmed, or unsure *what* to do; tracking what is going on in Body|Mind|World is *always* useful. After a while you will automatically take stock of what is going on in yourself (body and mind) and what is going on in your environment (world). Just this increase in your awareness will help you cope, express, manage, create, explore, and live more effectively.

Once you have the body, mind, world habit, you will find that you can apply it to almost any situation. Take your work, for example, when your boss gives you an assignment that you recognize as one of the tasks you least enjoy doing in your job. Start tracking body and mind to see what is happening. Are tensions making the body uncomfortable? Are there feelings (like self-pity and aversion) that are also making you emotionally uncomfortable? Are there thoughts in the mind that could be distorted by exaggeration or lack of understanding? Do conditions in the world make this assignment a challenge, like co-workers or equipment, or repetitive actions that bore you?

Some of these unpleasant sensations may be changeable (e.g. body tension, exaggeration, self-pity) and thereby take a big chunk of the discomfort out of the task. Remember the negativity bias we mentioned in the Nurture Positive exercise? I often suggest people make a mental note of body, mind, and world at the beginning of an unpleasant task and then again after it has been completed, to see if it was as bad as expected. About ninety percent of the time people say, "No, my concern in advance was much worse than what it really was like doing it." This is an example of that negativity bias producing a memory of the task that is more negative than the reality of it.

Let's use my work as a therapist as another example. I am paying attention and responding to multiple sensations the whole time I am working with someone. My client is basically my world (and also my meditation focus for an hour), but my own body and mind are also producing a lot of inner feelings and thoughts. Outwardly, I'm noticing the client's physical, verbal, and non-verbal behavior plus listening very carefully to the contents of what is said. Meanwhile, some of my awareness is also tracking all my inner experiences that are connected to the therapy relationship. As my mindfulness has developed, I am more able to stay centered and responsive despite quite a lot of distractions.

Direction

This strategy uses the directional nature of our attention to broaden the possibilities for responding to a situation. *Attention* is a cognitive process of selectively focusing on a particular sensory event and excluding others. Due to our brains' limited resources, we can pay attention to just one thing at a time. This one-thing-at-a-time limitation actually becomes a useful mindful awareness training strategy if we apply it intentionally.

Mindful awareness makes what is in front of us light up and become real and alive while other events fade into the background. We notice that when attention is "turned toward" a particular sensation, we are necessarily "turned away" from other sensations; we are unaware or only dimly aware of other things in the environment. One common example of this is our ability to listen to the conversation of one person at a party where many people's voices may be heard at once; our attention is turning toward one person and excluding all the other possible conversations. In BM we use both mindful turning toward and mindful turning away strategies to strengthen the attentional process and thus gain the benefits of being able to control our attention. What are the benefits of controlling attention? Here are some we will be exploring in depth.

Turning Toward Strategy: Simple Contact, Deconstruction into Manageable Size

Simple Contact means using attention as a way of *making contact with something*. We make contact with self and world: we "touch them," so to speak. Using mindful awareness, we turn toward an experience, make clear contact with it; we come to know it, learn about it, experience it, and accept it as it is. An important feature here is that *we absorb information from whatever we contact*. Part of the information absorbed is a feeling tone of pleasant, unpleasant, or neutral. Turning toward ourselves with mindful awareness, we gradually know and accept all of who/what we are more fully, including the feeling tone piece of information.

However, noticing the feeling tone can be both a gift and a curse. We humans are pretty much wired to turn toward life's pleasurable (preferred) conditions, and most of us expect that life will be better if we seek pleasurable feelings all the time. We want pleasure and not pain; respect and not blame; health and not illness; wealth and not poverty. We believe this will make us happy, all the while knowing deep down that we have to accept all experiences, both good and bad. Folk wisdom recognizes this tendency with sayings such as: "You have to take the bad with the good"; "What goes up must come down"; and "No pain, no gain." But the desire to have only the positive is so strong that at conscious and unconscious levels, much of our energy is directed to turning toward what we find are pleasurable conditions and away from the unpleasurable ones.

Mindful awareness helps us *accept all conditions and even be curious about them*: the good, the bad, the exciting, the boring. Mindful awareness is grounded in the deep understanding that all experience comes from the same Source and is valuable. We absorb information from all sensory experience, so if we resist unpleasurable kinds of contact, we also miss out on the information inherent in those experiences. All information has value and is significant for our deeper happiness and well-being. For example, there are constant reminders that everything in life is temporary and comes to an end, whether it is a meal, a movie, or our own mortal existence. But how often do we go through life acting as if an experience will go on forever? By expecting there will always be another meal, another movie, another day, we become numb to the meal, the movie, or the relationship in front of us *right now*. Instead of the complete experience (remember, that is a core practice goal), we have an incomplete experience of the meal, the movie, or the relationship.

An example of this is eating. We have all had the experience of being full but still taking another helping or ordering dessert, thus ignoring the knowledge in the mind that we have eaten a reasonable portion, or the sensations of fullness in the body. These mind/body sensations carry information; they are both *signals informing us that we have had enough food* and as such are very useful to our well-being. Ignoring them in the short term causes the discomfort of over-fullness, but ignoring them over the long run can cause serious health consequences.

Deconstruction is an action of mindful awareness that allows us to accept and observe (without reactivity) the displeasure, disappointment, or frustration when it is time to stop a pleasurable activity. How? By breaking things down into small enough pieces that we can have a complete experience. Take the food example. We know rationally that we have had enough food, but the mind (as talk) and the body (craving) might urge us on anyway. The talk might be saying: "This food tastes good; I want to taste it more; I want this pleasure to continue." The mind might also use images to picture the food in the mouth and its taste. The "wanting" part is the body's non-verbal emotional and physical sensations demanding rewarding brain chemicals such as dopamine and norepinephrine that are stimulated by eating. With the

Noting technique and core mindful awareness skills (concentration, clarity, equanimity) we can turn toward unpleasant experience (in this case the pain of denying more food). In other words, we stop resisting the disappointment or unmet craving, face it head on, then *deconstruct* it into smaller, more manageable pieces.

Using the eating example, we would pay attention to the food (world) and notice what part of the urge to eat it was in the body (desire, anticipation of pleasure, mouth-watering smells), and what part was in the mind (mental image of food, mental talk: "Go ahead; It tastes really good; We'll eat less tomorrow"), what part was in the world (the visual appearance and smell of the food). Tracking these events as simply "Feel In, Feel Out, See In, Hear In" or simply "Feel, Feel, See, Hear" moment to moment breaks up the overall "urge to eat" into smaller, more neutral, and manageable units. Eventually the urge subsides and we are not pulled toward food anymore.

When they are small enough, most any painful sensations can be experienced (and the information that comes with them absorbed). Notice I didn't say that sensations would *stop* being painful, simply that we can make the pain manageable with mindful awareness.

> → ***Rule of thumb****: Use* **turn toward** *when you want to contact, face, and/or deconstruct experience into smaller, more manageable pieces.*

Turning Away Strategies: Deconstruction, Grounding, and Reconstruction

Turning toward experience with mindful awareness is a key skill to master, especially when dealing with painful sensations. However, turning away skillfully is just as essential—we all need a break from discomfort sometimes! It is natural and healthy to get away from too much sensory stimulation or everyday discomfort, what we call "sensory challenges." Basic Mindfulness shows us how to get a break and turn away from sensory challenges while **still developing core mindful awareness skills.** Here are three ways to turn away from challenges:

Deconstruct and disengage from a challenge by focusing on Flow states (Easy Flow). This form of deconstruction is more like dissolving. It happens when we experience sensation at a deeper level and the challenge on the surface disappears. Flow is the movement or dynamic aspect that *lies behind* all apparently fixed experience. An obvious example is a field of wheat rippling in the wind. Looking simply at the movement: it appears fluid, a golden ocean wave; the individual stalks with solid wheat kernels attached disappear from our visual experience. With training and practice we can detect the F low that lies behind all apparently fixed experience—a painful emotion, a persistent backache, annoying sounds—and become so absorbed in the movement, energy, and vibration quality that there is no space and time in awareness for the experience in which the pain arises to become fixated into a thing.

Ground the bodymind sensation by focusing on restful states (Easy Rest) or anchoring in external sights and sounds (Focus on World). Feeling *grounded* means both that we are in and connected to sensations that make up the physical body and the physical world, including the actual ground. The earth and all things possessing solidity have the effect of stabilizing and renewing us. The ground gives us both nourishment and a solid, stable place to stand. Zen master Thich Nhat Hanh also emphasizes this principle with an exercise called "Touching the Earth"(1).

Reconstruct a positive sense of self by replacing negative sensations in body and mind with positive sensations (Nurture Positive). Just as focusing on particular kinds of restful states produces the sensations of grounding and tranquility that counterbalances conditions of bodymind stress and overactivity, likewise our ego (also called sense of self) is made up of certain bodymind sensations that bind together to create the sense of "I" or "me." When these self-referential sensations are negative, the sense of self is also negative in tone or content, i.e. we "feel" bad. This could be negative self-talk or beliefs in the mind, negative emotions, or physical sensations in the body. The purpose of *reconstruction* is to cultivate positive mind and body sensations in order to replace the negative ones. Doing this, our intention is to "turn away from negative" by actively using "turn toward positive." When we use mindful awareness to strategically fill it with positive thoughts and feelings, there is little room left for negatives to enter our awareness. Shinzen often says, "There is only so much real estate in consciousness"(2)

> → **Rule of thumb:** *Use the **turn away** strategy when you want to deconstruct by dissolving into flow, are needing rest and stabilization through grounding, or want to reconstruct experience by replacing negative thoughts and feelings with more positive or rational ones.*

There are examples of deconstruction, grounding, and reconstruction in the case studies offered later in this section.

Other Benefits of Turn Toward and Turn Away

Turning attention toward or away with mindful awareness optimizes the impact of our attention in at least three ways:

- Sensations are constantly flowing at and through us, which is a challenge. By turning toward and away from sensations with mindful awareness, we accept (rather than resist) the flow of experience. Acceptance allows a more satisfying connection with and a more thoughtful response to any sensations. With acceptance, sensory events can seem to flow through us rather than feeling like they are colliding with us.

- Sometimes sensory experiences fill our consciousness in a way that seems we have become the sensation itself. For example, when we say things like "I **am** sad," we have turned toward the emotion of sadness to the point of merging with it; it becomes "who we are" momentarily. Merging with thoughts and emotions tends to happen unconsciously, but we can also intentionally turn to something *in order to merge with it and temporarily become it*—a pleasant feeling, a happy thought, a cloud, beautiful music, flowing water, and so on.

- Over time, these natural turning actions become habits, then those habits become lifestyles. *When mindfulness controls the turns* (as opposed to distraction or avoidance) *then mindfulness becomes a lifestyle and we are less often caught in destructive habits or hijacked by momentary impulses.* When we **turn toward** sensations using mindfulness, we make challenges easier to digest, reduce the suffering involved, gain insight, and accept ourselves as we are. When we **turn away** from sensations with mindfulness, we renew ourselves in restful experience and replace negative identities and preferences with a positive sense of self. We also learn to optimize actions we can take when challenged.

ION – Interest, Opportunity, Necessity

Because there are so many options, one of the most frequent questions I get when teaching Basic Mindfulness is which technique to practice. We are taught this acronym, ION, which stands for "interest," "opportunity," and "necessity." If there is no specific need or challenge facing us then we can simply choose what *interests* us. Perhaps we want to explore the body or even just emotional-type sensations in the body. Maybe we want to go by modalities and try just "See", just "Hear", just "Feel". Perhaps we are interested in perfecting our ability to relax the body at will. Perhaps we want to contrast inward sensations with outward sensations. Or maybe we feel we need more practice being present to our world—the external sights of our environment. The system allows you to explore almost any meditation focus you could be interested in using.

The second circumstance that might direct what we choose to practice is *opportunity*. An example might be your family members are all away, you are home alone, and so it is more possible to explore listening to silence. Or, perhaps as you were practicing noting the physical sensation of the breath, and you suddenly experienced those sensations as movement or waves coursing through the body. You recognize this as an opportunity to explore Flow and shift your focus from the ordinary somatic sensation of the body ("Feel Out") to the dynamic movement quality of the body, using "Feel Flow" labeling. (If you were using the one-word label "Feel," this shift is only simply in *what your attention is focused on*. You still use the "Feel" label, but now you are clear with yourself that you have moved from physical sensation in the body to Flow in the body.)

Sometimes we are choosing techniques because there are emotional and physical challenges that simply **demand** our attention: we have no choice. We must face them out of *necessity*. So we use a technique that fits the situation and the demand. Here is a funny example:

I was attending a Basic Mindfulness retreat with Shinzen. If you have never attended a retreat like this, there is a meditation period when the teacher (or a person designated to sub in for him) sits in the front facing the entire group of meditators. They ring the bell to start and end the sit and otherwise be a strong example for everyone of sitting upright, being still, silent, and concentrated for the meditation period.

Master teachers are very inspiring to watch as they meditate, and Shinzen is no exception. Even in long meditations (two hours or so) if you open your eyes periodically, he always appears serene, content, and immovable.

Shinzen was leading this particular sit and it was the sitting period before he was to give an evening dharma talk. It was a hot summer night in Southern California with no air conditioning, which can make sitting still much more difficult. I remember looking at Shinzen a number of times and feeling admiration for how calm and statuesque he was.

Later that night just before the dharma talk, he mentioned that he had begun to sweat at the start of the meditation and it happened that some tiny insect had found the moisture on his ear to be very satisfying. He had us all in tears of laughter as he described the insect crawling in, out, all around his ear over and over for the whole period. Then he said, "This was one of those times when I thought I might meditate in one way, but due to necessity, in order to maintain my sanity and be still, my only option was to concentrate completely on the trail of this tiny insect, moment to moment. No attention to thoughts, no attention to emotions or external sounds, no deep rapture. My entire meditation was following a little fly."

One major realization I came to was that *absolutely anything* we experience can help us deepen mindful awareness. This made a profound impression on me.

ATTITUDE

When my daughter was little, we would occasionally have this conversation:

"Mom, I want you to come *be* with me."

"But honey, I'm right here, doing the dishes while you read. I *am* with you."

"*No.* I want you to come *here* and *beeee* with me."

I think we can all understand what she was saying. She wanted me to stop paying attention to anything else and be present to her, to give my full attention to her. Usually this did not mean doing anything special, she simply wanted me to be interested in her and make contact with her. This simple act was deeply important to her, enough so that she would ask for it much like she would ask for something she liked to eat. One of the hallmarks of interpersonal mindfulness—offering acceptance and being truly present in the moment with people—is that they enjoy us even if we aren't "doing" anything special! We can enjoy attending to ourselves in the same way. Simply "being with" our experience rather than always expecting, doing, evaluating our experience is a self-accepting way of attending to ourselves.

Up until now we have spoken of mindfulness as a training program with goals. Paradoxically, "being-rather-than-doing" can facilitate change when intended action does not. Lao Tzu was perhaps the first to clearly articulate this twenty-six centuries ago when he said, "The way to do is to be" (3). Truly being present with our own sensory experience (or that of others) allows us to see and embrace reality as it is.

Mindfulness can be infused with an attitude of acceptance: making deep contact with sensory experience and letting events be as they are. Or, mindfulness can be infused with an attitude of change: experiments in changing ourselves, changing something in the world. To mature as human beings we need to appreciate, transcend, and improve self and world (4).

Even though we use the same Basic Mindfulness attentional skill training for all three jobs, we may have a *different attitude* depending upon which job we are focused on in the moment. Appreciating self and world requires us to bring an attitude of *acceptance*. Transcending or improving self and world both require us to bring an attitude of *change*. Sometimes we choose mindfulness as an acceptance strategy for self and world; sometimes we choose mindfulness as a change strategy for self and world.

Acceptance: Mindfulness as Presence and Appreciation

What happens when we apply the acceptance strategy of presence to our own sensory experience, i.e. we "be with" whatever we are experiencing? It simultaneously becomes both an activity that is a teaching tool and the mindful awareness that is the activity resulting from the teaching. As we "be with" ourselves we make simple contact with arising sensations, focusing attention on them with equanimity (remember, equanimous means neither grasping nor pushing away). There is not the push to "do'" anything with sensations; rather, they are allowed to arise and leave as they will. We are noticing details of them when they are present and making contact with the particular sensation without acting or responding. In doing this we are:

- developing mindful awareness skills of concentration, clarity, and equanimity
- understanding pure mindfulness as "being with" our sensory experience.
- growing an attitude of acceptance, friendliness, appreciation, and inclusion for all of our experience by welcoming everything that arises
- allowing the opportunity for completion of experience and flow to occur

Acceptance is a way of appreciating things as they are, deeply allowing life to be the way it is. Making no changes means we neither resist events nor grasp and fixate on them. It is a coping strategy that permits the flow of nature to pass through us.

Change: Mindfulness as Curiosity, Experimentation, and Transformation

The second activity my daughter absolutely loved to share with me was something we called "science experiments." An experiment might consist of my simultaneously applying light stroking on her arm or leg or tummy and with fake sternness insisting she not laugh lest she "ruin the experiment." Or I would slowly work my fingers around each of her toes with the "boring worm," an imaginary instrument that in fact was my finger! I would feign a stern scientist face and say something like: "No, this is serious business. We are doing science here and trying to see just how much tickle you can absorb or how far the boring worm can crawl without you laughing. Very important work." Naturally, this illusion of her mother as serious scientist created tension (like the tension of a carnival ride) and even greater fun and laughter at the end of the game.

Another way we practice mindfulness is by experimenting with the sensations that arise. If, much like a scientist, we adopt an attitude of curiosity and experimentation, then we are free to 1) express curiosity about how our experience and sensations interact; 2) take specific actions regarding what we experience; and 3) see what the overall impact is on our experience. Are things better in the body, mind, world? Worse? No change? We take a strategic action in the interest of triggering one of the beneficial results, such as reduced physical or emotional suffering, increased physical or emotional satisfaction, insight, behavioral change, and so forth. Approaching our experience with an experimental attitude enables us to be goal-directed but with lighthearted curiosity and a sense of no-fault exploration. The experience is evaluated in the sense of noticing whether the *impact* is positive, negative, or neutral. We are not using the outcome of the experience to categorize or pathologize ourselves.

For example, when trying an experiment with mental talk, we may find that by turning attention to it in a particular way, the talk disappears temporarily. We are not "good" or "cured" or "better" as a person for this. Rather, we have learned something about the interactions of sensory experience. "When I do this, that happens." This may seem like common sense, but it is also called "insight into sensory interactions." With insight our behavior can change and our life conditions then may become better, leading to increased satisfaction.

Some other change experiments are:
- work to find, create, enhance, or minimize sensations rather than simply letting them arise and be as they are
- direct attention to contrasting sensations such as active versus rest; inner versus outer; parts versus wholes, body versus mind; turn toward versus turn away, be with versus experiment with
- restrict our awareness to a particular sensation and track it over time for particular qualities such as content, intensity, duration, frequency, complexity

There are also times when simple acceptance can be the change needed. Not long ago I was working with a meditation student, Lou, who is devoted to his Jewish heritage and religion but finds himself resisting his family because they are controlling and judgmental of him. His interest in exploring Buddhism and dating women outside of his faith always triggered a big fight with his parents. They were also angry that he moved to the West coast, as far from them as he could. Lou was in therapy with a colleague to work on these and other issues but was coming to me for mindfulness training. He had learned to track body, mind, and world, plus some Nurture Positive exercises.

One day Lou started talking about an argument with his parents and how he didn't think they would ever change their attitudes and he would never want to be around them if they didn't. At that time he was seriously dating a Christian woman and couldn't really speak with his parents about this big part of his life, plus he felt guilty about doing something he knew would upset them. Lou found himself ruminating a great deal about this dilemma and said the worrying limited his choices. He asked how he could use mindfulness to deal with it.

I said, "If your parents are not changing, maybe you could learn to accept the physical and emotional feelings in your body as well as thoughts in the mind that occur when your life choices upset them. I mean, if things cannot change, you might as well just live your life the way you believe you should, accept yourself, accept them and their reactions. Sort of live deeply with it *as it is* rather than imagining a way to change anything." He liked this idea and I had him practice imagining their reactions in his mind and then tracking (noting) the responses in his body. I suggested he acknowledge and accept the current situation deeply, by both tracking it in this way and then offering self-compassion to himself and his parents as another exercise.

Lou returned a few months later because he was moving back east for his job and he wanted to say goodbye. His first words were: "It really helped me when you said, 'Live with it' and then showed how tracking body and mind could do that. I had always thought 'about' their upsetness but had not tried to live through it. And you know what? I just attended Easter dinner with my girlfriend! Can you believe that, Passover one day and Easter the next? I never could have done that the way I felt before."

For Lou, it was liberating to learn he could live with his feelings and his parents' feelings rather than worry about changing them. He was freer to be himself and choose his own way through the complications of modern life. But sometimes we really need to make changes, like when our health depends on it and life circumstances require a new approach.

When I teach acceptance and change as coping skills, I often use the terms "be with" and "experiment with" to describe acceptance and change options. However, according to more traditional Buddhist systems for training mindfulness, acceptance is seen as the purest mindfulness training. They argue that trying to interfere with the way things arise spontaneously may be necessary but is not mindfulness training. But there are meditation teachers who tell us that both ways are important(5). My teacher says it like this: "Sometimes it is time to bear down, make effort, and sometimes it is time to ease up, do nothing. It is important to have significant contrasts when working with consciousness"(6).

I agree that the contrast of doing both acceptance and change is invaluable for me personally and in my work with students and clients. We learn something from sitting and appreciating things as they are, and we learn something quite different when we play with things, poke at them, move them around, and see what happens. The contrast of the two learnings can produce invaluable wisdom and/or relief. With some regularity, especially with feelings that overwhelm, I will have students alternate between "be with" (acceptance) and "experiment with" (change) regarding their experience.

It is tempting to ask which the best way is. If I had to choose only one of these, I would agree with the traditionalists and just teach acceptance. In my experience, nothing can change if it cannot first be accepted, and often acceptance leads to the change that is wanted. However, my deeper experience is that both are necessary. The phrase "no pain, no gain" points to the learning that comes from doing things the hard way, the painful way. Zen practice expresses this value when it encourages students to be completely still during sitting, no matter what discomfort they feel. It is called "strong determination" and from this practice one can learn important lessons about the bodymind and living with pain. However, there is also something to be learned from adjusting posture when in pain, eating instead of denying certain foods, or even ending a job or relationship rather than persisting with it. Sometimes we must take action to make our conditions better and experiments help us to learn skillful action. Experimenting looks at effects of and interactions between sensory events.

> → **Rule of thumb**: *Alternate between "mindfulness as appreciation" and "mindfulness as change" to both embrace and try to change overwhelming emotions.*

DO WHAT WORKS!

Regardless of what strategy(s) you choose, if things are not working, be flexible and change your approach. Keep trying something else in the Toolkit. By "not working" we mean either: 1) you cannot *do* the particular exercise for some reason; or 2) you are not getting any of the benefits that naturally accompany mindfulness practice, such as:

- managing daily challenges
- increasing daily satisfaction
- boosting self-and-world awareness
- changing behavior

When I lead clients through a meditation, they will often say something like: "This isn't working. I'm not any calmer or happier. I just notice how much my mind keeps judging things and now I'm more aware that I feel sad and ashamed each time that happens." Because their emotions are negative, they "feel" negative about the meditation and truly believe that things are not working, when in fact they are gaining clarity and insight into their body and mind. THINGS ARE WORKING JUST FINE! It is unfortunately true that at the beginning of learning mindfulness we more frequently encounter negative sensations than positive ones. This is because our unconscious (unmindful) way of relating to experience is usually to either push it away (suppression) or become identified with it (fusion). When with successful mindfulness practice we begin relating to *all* experience without suppression or identification, the first sensations to come into awareness are often the ones we have habitually pushed away, i.e. negative sensations.

Another complaint that often occurs is: "I keep looking, but I'm not noticing anything; nothing is coming up; it's all quiet and still." Again, the person sees a problem because of their expectation of a **particular outcome.** In fact, something very important happens "when nothing is happening": the body is relaxed and/or the mind is blank and quiet. This is a restful state and always good for our mental and physical health. If we keep doing the practice, regardless of how it feels in the moment, sooner or later we will see benefits even if they're not the ones we expected. And if nothing else, any strategy and exercise in the Basic Mindfulness Toolkit is training mindfulness **at the same time** you are working to accomplish your particular goals.

Chapter Five

Challenges That Focus Our Attention

While almost any exercise you choose is likely to be helpful, it is important for you **to make a clear and intentional decision at the outset about what to work on and how to work on it. Then choose an exercise from the BMT and set the intention to pay attention to that focus for the duration of the exercise.** While systems of psychotherapy prefer to use formal diagnostic categories as the focus for mindfulness training (7), there is no requirement to have a diagnosis to be able to choose a mindfulness exercise for general training or to work through challenging events. We don't have to be sick to want to practice mindfulness!

When I started applying mindfulness in psychotherapy twenty years ago, I used the clients' immediate complaints and symptoms (challenges) as a guide. What was happening *now* that we could apply mindfulness to? In the Basic Mindfulness Toolkit, I use categories based on the ordinary kinds of challenges that show up most often in my office. As you read through these you should ask yourself: What is grabbing my attention right *now*? Locate which challenge is the most relevant at this moment. Just as I found the Body|Mind|World categories easier and more intuitive for describing sensory experience, I find the following challenge categories more intuitive for people as well. So although I developed this approach in the practice of psychotherapy, I prefer talking about experience and teaching mindfulness in a language that gets away from the pathologizing language of medicine.

Here are the challenge categories I have found most useful:

DIFFICULT EMOTIONS AND/OR PHYSICAL SENSATIONS

After the homeostatic needs of survival (e.g. food, sleep, reproduction), difficult emotions and physical pain are perhaps the most basic challenges that humans face, and certainly ones for which mindfulness offers great help. In fact, some studies suggest that conditions of disordered emotional states such as depression and anxiety are involved for ninety percent of the people who present for medical and psychological treatment. As life flows through us we either have some primary affective (sensory) experience (like anger, fear, sadness) or a secondary emotional reaction mediated by mental constructs (jealousy, resentment, anticipatory fears, etc.). Secondary emotions happen in response to something else and can appear as a story in the mind. Secondary emotional reactions are how suffering takes place and are especially present in humans because of their large brains and ability to "think about" what is happening to them. These reactions are also a key feature of chronic pain. Even small amounts of physical and/or emotional pain, when combined, can trigger the sensation that we are overwhelmed.

> → ***Rule of thumb:*** *Use a "deconstruction" strategy when there is the perception of "too much" of something (overwhelm) going on.*

BEHAVIOR CHANGE

In addition to wanting help with emotions, behavior change is probably the #2 problem we all face. Something we are doing or not doing either helps us survive and thrive or stands in the way of surviving and thriving. Maladaptive inner behaviors such as urges, thoughts, and intentions may be pushing maladaptive outer behaviors such as actions or words. When you look at the definition of the word "urge," you find that as a noun it means something like "strong restless desire"; as a verb, "to force or impel, to push for something." Urges are the emotions, desires, or unseen forces within us that push us to take action, most of the time to do what will keep us alive as a species, like eating, sleeping, sex, and so on. But these same urges can be problematic for us as individuals, compelling us to overdo things—eat too much or too little, drink too much alcohol, gamble, have unprotected sex. There are also urges to turn away from certain feelings or activities resulting in procrastination or avoidance. It is sometimes helpful to see the problem of urges as "too much turn toward" or "too much turn away," then select a mindfulness exercise that either offers balance in the other direction or deep clarification of the urge itself (i.e. practice with an acceptance attitude before trying to change anything).

We seek changes in our inner experience and actions in the world. Behavior change has already been noted as a natural byproduct of training mindful awareness (see Part One) and therefore is a natural goal for mindfulness practice.

> → **Rule of thumb:** *Use an attitude of "acceptance" when something stands in the way of the desired goal and you cannot see clearly what it is. Repeated simple contact over time yields more clarity (resolution power) and deeper insight into what is needed for change to occur.*

> → **Rule of thumb:** *Clarify the Body|Mind|World components of the urge and track them over time to increase tolerance-without-action for the sensations and insight into impermanence of sensations (urge-surfing).*

STRESS

"Stress reduction" is probably one of the most common goals people list when asked why they are seeking psychotherapy or mindfulness training. Rest, physical and mental renewal, as well as engaging our "play" system are critical to overall health and well-being. During this decreased-activity-down-time our minds store memory, our physical bodies repair tissues, and the immune system renews itself. Mindfulness can be a critical aid to reducing stress, inducing rest states, and inviting the natural recovery process to function. And, it just feels good! Many people learn mindfulness skills because it's pleasurable to disconnect from the feeling of *Go! Go! Go!* all the time, even when the going is pleasurable activity.

While negative emotions can be involved with stress and vice versa, I differentiate stress from category #1 "Difficult Emotions and/or Physical Sensations" by the fact of *quantity* being the critical factor in "stress" (*too much* pleasant or unpleasant activity), and the *qualities* of negativity (angry, fearful, sad, panicky, burning, sharp, throbbing, etc.) being the more salient features of "Difficult Emotions and/or Physical Sensations."

> → ***Rule of thumb:*** *Try a "turn away" strategy temporarily when there is "too much" of something going on (overwhelm) or simply use a "deconstruction" strategy.*

SENSE OF SELF ISSUES

If life is composed of sensory input, then who experiences all these sensations? Who is the "I, me, my" we are referring to when we say "**I** feel pain" or "That belongs to **me**" or "You hurt **my** feelings'?" or "**I** want (don't want) that"? We call that "I" our "self," and it is actually made up of sensory experiences. (Sounds weird, maybe, but it's true.) Certain thoughts, emotions, and body sensations combine to create the feeling that you have a continuous and separate "self" that "feels" things in the bodymind and "initiates" action in the world.

If you try to look and find a self in the body or mind, you can't. It's simply body activity (emotional and physical sensations) plus mind activity (mental images and mental talk) combining into the illusion of a "self" and interacting with world sensations (sights and sounds) that seem to be external to that self. Moment to moment there is a Body|Mind|World interaction that feels continuous enough to be a fixed entity we call "self" (similar to how a motion picture appears as a continuous picture but is actually a series of discrete shots rapidly flashed on a screen). This constructed self is not really a fixed and separate thing (even though it feels that way); rather, it is a series of sensations that must combine fluidly to make the sense there is a reliable 'self' doing the experiencing. We call this the sense of self (or sometimes self-sense) and might compare it to sense of touch or sense of hearing. (**Note:** the terms "sense of self" and "self-sense" are used synonymously here.)

The sense of self is not present at birth but develops with experiential contact and maturation. There are several functions that the sense of self performs:

- **Contain and regulate primary sensory experiences passing through the bodymind system–** The self-sense acts as a psychological container, i.e. a holder, for physical and emotional sensations passing through it. As infants, we don't feel ourselves to be separate from our caregivers and world; we rely on those caregivers to modulate our emotions and satisfy physical demands. As we mature the sense of "I am" as separate from the caregiver develops and begins to take over these self-care and self-soothing functions. As we mature even more, the complexities of our social environment (education, relationships, work) require a more complex and skillful bodymind regulation system. The self-sense grows and evolves to adapt to these growing demands.

- **Interact with the world and other "selves" in it**– We humans cannot survive in the world alone. We separate from caregivers and develop self-care skills, but we are social animals and require safe connections (attachment) with others for our entire lives. To do this, self must learn to balance group needs with individual needs. This balancing requires social skills (reading verbal and non-verbal cues), communication skills (language and conflict resolution), and a certain amount of flexibility.

- **Maintain conventional (shared) reality**– The self must be realistic in its appraisal of itself and others, such that a shared understanding among the various selves is possible. Specifically, the subjective self is made of mental images, mental talk, and the physical and emotional body. This subjective (inner) self experiences the objective (outer) world as sights and sounds, including the sights and sounds that make up objects and other people in the world.

In order to have shared reality we have to agree with others about what is there. If I see a tree and want to talk about it, but no one else sees the tree, I'm not sharing that part of external reality with another. Similarly, if I hold the view of myself (inner images and talk) that I am a kind person but cannot find someone else who agrees with that based on my external behavior, being kind is not a shared view. Conventional reality is also consensual, i.e. it consists of those things we can agree on.

- **Maintain flexible boundaries**– The constructed self needs to permit new contents to flow in and old to flow out. Again, the self is made of mental images, mental talk, and the emotional and physical body. With this constructed self we play many roles in life—child, parent, employee, student, lover, teacher—and each of these requires a different self with different bodymind components. So we must be able to allow old self-parts to flow out and new ones to flow in. But, we have to do this without boundaries becoming so loose that the self cannot do its container function anymore and know itself as separate from others. Overly loose boundaries create problems of holding and managing emotions or distinguishing our own feelings and desires from those of other people.

The self-sense experiences sensations that seem external to it (the world), but it can also experience itself: what we typically call being "self-aware." Sometimes being self-aware is negative, as when we feel self-conscious. Other times being self-aware is positive, like when we feel proud or competent in some way. The sense of self is *not fixed but feels as if it is* to the user, and this illusion can create problems in the formation and use of the sense of self. There is a certain "feel" to the changing nature of the self that is sometimes exciting and sometimes scary. I remember noticing this in elementary school at the end of each school year. Usually I was happy in my classroom with work and friends, liked my teacher, and felt liked by him/her. Basically I "knew how to do" that grade and felt competent. At the close of the year I was sad to have that all come to an end, and occasionally worried about the future. Maybe the next year wouldn't be as good as this one; what if I wouldn't be able to "learn how to do" that next year because it was too hard for me? At the same time, if you had asked if I just wanted to stay in third grade, I would have been horrified, because I so much wanted to experience what I saw "upper graders" doing.

I recognize now that what I was feeling was the sense of self losing the set of thoughts and feelings that formed my third grade self in order for another set of thoughts and feelings to flow in and form my fourth grade self. If I resist this natural flow, or the conditions in my world are not supportive of the flow process, the formation of the self does not happen smoothly. In some cases the sense of self may not function as well for the next role required or future changes imposed by the flow of events.

The many ways for the sense of self to form itself create challenges. Even when our sense of self is stable and functions well, we still feel these challenges to some extent over the course of a lifetime; it is all a matter of degree. Here are a few obvious ones:

Too Solid

The sense of self is experienced too solidly and prevents new bodymind experiences from replacing one another. Overly rigid boundaries keep the self-sense fixed in one role or one set of ideas about life. This lack of flexibility, release, and renewal renders the self vulnerable to problems of rigidity. The result could be compulsive or ritualistic behavior, obsessive or rigid thinking, inability to adapt to change, futile efforts to control the future, etc. Another feature of the rigid sense of self is that it produces too strong a notion of "I, me, and mine." We become over-identified with thoughts and feelings and problems of possessiveness, jealousy, or feeling threatened by others.

Too Loose

The sense of self combines too loosely and bodymind components flow too quickly or chaotically to make the sense of self arise in a stable fashion. Overly loose boundaries can result in problems of holding and managing emotions or distinguishing our own feelings and desires from those of other people. Such a self is vulnerable to emotional volatility because it isn't a strong enough container to hold emotions as they flow through. The diffuseness of this sense of self also makes it difficult to know "self" from "other," i.e. we can't tell if what we're feeling belongs to us or the other person(s). Finally, indecisiveness and confusion can occur when there is not a stable self-sense. We can't locate what "I' like, what "I" want, how "I" feel.

Distortions

The sense of self is based on distortions in the mind or body. The distortions can be mental beliefs born out of mistaken understandings of childhood (e.g. believing one is unworthy and/or lacking something because parents were neglectful or absent). The distortion can be something that is mostly body, like being fearful of all dogs because you were scared by a dog at some point. The sense of self becomes "someone who is afraid of dogs." The distortions can be body or mind sensations that are not consistent with external reality, like somatic, visual, and auditory hallucinations.

Lack of Integration

The mind and body aspects of the sense of self are not integrated in some way. In this situation the mind may think one way and the body feel another. In trauma situations, the lack of integration is often both in the mind and body The body "knows" something that is not known conceptually to the mind and "speaks" using body symptoms such as anxiety and depression, chronic headaches or stomachaches, tension, soreness, or frequent injury of back, legs, neck.

Being human, we all have some of the too tight, too loose, distortion, lack of integration qualities in our sense of self. When they are pronounced, they affect everyday functioning.

PERSONAL DEVELOPMENT AND RENEWAL

Many times the goal isn't related to a challenge but is simply to deepen our ability to be present to our experience. Mindful awareness training has been compared to a gym workout for the physical body. With strategic and regular practice, we are doing a "consciousness workout." The exercises for Body|Mind|World enable us to develop consciousness in several ways:

- Emotionally, we are able to observe experience but suspend taking action, thus increasing our tolerance for emotional arousal. With increased emotional tolerance, we are able to make more reasoned decisions and take more reasoned actions, which leads to better functioning in the world.
- Physically we move toward reducing stress states of the body. "Fight/flight" responses of the nervous system are more quickly replaced with "rest, digest, nurture" responses in which rest and recovery of the body take place.
- Psychologically the deconstruction of the sense of self into its constituent parts helps us truly experience our fluid and impermanent nature, increasing wisdom. Enhancing restful states grounds and anchors our sense of self, making it something we can rely on despite its fluid and impermanent nature. Finally, using Nurture Positive we reconstruct the sense of self with more rational or optimistic Body|Mind|World components. Shinzen often remarks, "All of these practices working together make the 'self' a home rather than a prison"(8).

Personal development is why some people may start mindfulness training, but many are drawn to it as a contemplative practice. In doing so we train to refine the personal aspect of ourselves so that it becomes sensitive to a universal dimension: God, Spirit, Allah, Source, etc. I mentioned earlier that according to Basic Mindfulness, the main personal jobs we all have as humans are: appreciating self and world, getting over the self and world, improving self and world. Mindfulness practice is a key tool for doing these jobs.

Naturally, you might have a lot of other kinds of challenges or goals not mentioned here. These are not meant to represent the only kinds of challenges you face but are just a selection that I encounter often in myself and in my students. You are free to use other sensory experiences as your focus.

When your goal is personal development and renewal, the decision about what exercise to do is wide open. Even if you learn just one exercise and one strategy and do it regularly, you will reap benefits. Those of you who are more ambitious might spend some time with each of the six BMT tools so that you learn all the strategies mentioned in this book.

Chapter Six

Two Questions to Get Started

The last two chapters have outlined general guidelines for applying mindful awareness strategies to everyday life as well as to some of the challenges most everyone faces sooner or later. Our final step is to combine the challenge we are facing and the preference to turn toward or away from that challenge. We do that by simply asking two questions to establish what our challenge is and whether we feel like facing it or not right now.

QUESTION#1: WHAT IS MY CHALLENGE FOCUS FOR THIS PRACTICE TIME?

Sometimes we know exactly what we want to focus on because it's already screaming and tugging for our attention. You know this kind of experience; maybe it's something physically uncomfortable or emotionally painful. Our attention is naturally drawn to pay attention to pain as a survival mechanism. Sometimes, though, it is not one thing in particular, but instead our response to the "too muchness" of everyday life that we feel pushed to focus on. Recently someone said to me, "I think I'm suffering from death by to-do list." However, there are also times when our meditation focus is not so obvious.

In any event, I find that paying close attention to "What part of my experience is in the body? What part is in the mind? What part arises in the world?" is a useful strategy to start with. "What am I seeing?

What am I hearing? What am I feeling?" is another way to approach experience, by looking closely at sensory modalities that make up body, mind, and world.

Sometimes ordinary conversations and daily events will reveal something happening in body, mind, or world that would be useful to explore. Feelings that arise, mental images, and mental conversations about the past or future, comments people make–all suggest things you might explore mindfully. For example, I was recently planning a remodel and had the idea of removing a gas fireplace from my living room to create more space. Fireplaces are given special value when buying and selling homes, so I felt ambivalent about this destructive decision. I spoke to the contractors, designers, friends, and family, but it wasn't until someone looked at me quizzically and said, "*Janet, you are you having a hard time deciding this, aren't you?*" that I realized I needed to give it more focused mindful consideration.

That night it became my challenge focus during meditation. I spent the whole period noticing what was happening in the body and mind and world about it. It was surprising (but helpful) to discover how much fear-based thinking I had and the impact of this thinking on my decision-making. The ambivalence dropped off markedly just from seeing and feeling it all with deep clarity. All decisions involve some risk and I was willing to accept that regarding my remodel.

Most of your challenges or personal development opportunities will fall into the six challenge focus categories that were described earlier. Paying attention to events in Body|Mind|World (what you see, hear, feel) and using that list, you can target a challenge focus with which to use mindfulness.

QUESTION #2: DO I WANT TO TURN TOWARD OR AWAY FROM THE CHALLENGE?

After identifying the challenge focus you need to be clear whether you want to concentrate on the challenge at the present time or direct attention away from the challenge. Remember, we don't have the option of turning away from challenges forever; that would simply be avoidance and only make things worse in the long run. Both are necessary for growth and healthy adjustment. Turning away mindfully is an adaptation to challenges that we benefit from. Turning toward challenges is how we learn to live with and process both the pleasant and unpleasant experiences that are a natural expression of life. Knowing *how and when* to turn toward or away is ultimately a function of wisdom, but practicing both, we gradually gain insight into our own personality and what is best.

2A. *Turn toward* a challenge means we face it directly using the noting technique to track what is going on moment to moment in the body and mind. Two benefits we can maximize turning toward a challenge using noting are simple contact and deconstruction.

Simple contact helps us clarify, understand, experience deeply, and accept what is present (as opposed to what appears to be present). We may not realize it, but we can have many ideas or expectations about how an exercise should go and what we would feel. These expectations and ideas stand between us and the direct experience of our body. So if, for example, I am making simple contact with my body, my attention is curious about what is physically and emotionally present. I allow my attention to penetrate every sensation, absorb whatever information is presented by that sensation, appreciate the sensations as part of my aliveness-right-now. If I have had ideas about what my body *should* be feeling, I notice those as what they are, ideas-about-the-body rather than direct experience of the body, and return to the direct experience.

The unique feature of simple contact is that even though it is simple, it's also one of the most profound and transcendent contemplative practices I use. The metaphor I like to use for describing the power of simple contact is the sun. The sun does not choose to shine on "this and not that"; it reveals *everything* in its path. When we make simple contact, in any modality, awareness is simply bringing light (or sound or feeling) to the situation; painful or not, beautiful or not, everything is perfectly equal in awareness. Everything is revealed of its own accord, and we are not trying to add to or take anything from the experience.

Such contact also has remarkable power to heal as well as reveal. When we are willing to contact things as they are (as opposed to suppressing, avoiding, or distorting them), we start to loosen the blockages that limit us in some way. As we feel less blocked, energy is freed up to be more present to all of life. We feel lighter.

The exercises we use to make simple contact most often are:
- Focus on Body
- Focus on Mind
- Focus on World

Though we use these exercises more frequently to experience simple contact, we can experience its benefit with any of the exercises. For example, if you were doing Easy Rest or Easy Flow, you might still hold awareness on the rest and flow states with the "just reveal what is there" intention of simple contact. With Nurture Positive I like to make simple contact with whatever is triggered by the mind contents I have created. That is to say, the mental image and/or talk may produce pleasant or awkward or threatening feelings, but I greet them with simple contact regardless.

Deconstruction has the benefit of untangling the solidness of the story and feelings into the mental talk, mental image, emotional and physical body sensations from which they come.

The challenge is happening in the mind and/or the body so the exercises we would use in turning toward a challenge are:
- Focus on Body
- Focus on Mind

When I want the benefit of deconstructing experience, I focus awareness with the intention of experiencing one thing at a time. It is usually the mind that is creating a narrative about what is scaring the body, subsequently triggering more narrative in the mind. We disengage this narrative-body interaction by breaking things into their different, smaller parts: what is body; what is mind; what is world? Or alternately, what do I see; what do I hear; what do I feel? Or, perhaps even more narrowly, what do I feel in just my breath, *this* breath? By doing this I am able to manage the whole experience effectively. By concentrating on smaller and smaller individual strands of sensation, the larger whole ceases to exist so solidly as a thing.

2B. *Turn away* from a challenge means exactly what it says—we take a break from the challenge and then return sometime later to work directly on the challenge. But taking a break from the challenge does not mean taking a break from mindfulness. We *can turn away from the challenge mindfully* by choosing three possible beneficial effects: **grounding, deconstruction (using flow), or reconstruction.**

Grounding means being connected to our body and to the earth. The benefit of this connection is the sense of their solidity that makes us feel secure, tranquil, and stabilized. We can promote grounding with these exercises:
- Easy Rest (to increase the sense of peace and tranquility)

- Focus on World (to anchor in the solidity of the external world and get away from the challenge in the body and mind)

When using the Focus on World technique, it can enhance the grounding benefit to actually touch the ground or some other stable worldly object. The stability of the earth and trees and rocks is transmitted non-verbally to the body and confirmed by the concentrated awareness on the inherent stability.

Deconstruction using flow means dissolving the solid "something-ness" of sensations (e.g. fear of some future event) into simpler, less person-oriented sensory experiences. For example, instead of honing in on the story of the fearful event, we can focus in detail on the movement quality of the emotions throbbing in our chests, the breath as it moves the chest up and down, or the overall level of vibratory sensation in the body that accompanies strong emotions. This process is like deconstruction by breaking things into smaller pieces, except we attend to the underlying energy or force *behind* the surface experience of mind or body distress. We look *through* the surface distress to the deeper energies that push on and flow through us. The exercise we would use to turn away and deconstruct is:

- Easy Flow

Reconstruction is very much like cognitive behavior therapy (CBT) in that it replaces painful, irrational, or mistaken thoughts and feelings with pleasant, rational, or correct ones. So, for example, we could have negative mind components, such as mental images of ourselves getting nervous about speaking in public, or worrisome mental talk – "What if I forget? What if my mind goes blank? What if I bore them?" These in turn cause negative body sensations (fear, anxiety, tension in jaw and gut). With a reconstruction strategy, we replace the mental images and mental talk in the mind with pleasant, rational, or correct ones: images of prior successful speaking experiences and soothing mental talk – "It will go fine. You always start feeling a little nervous, but it never stays that way."

The concentration to hold the new components in mind, plus the clarity of focus on details of the impact they have on the body, are what *make this practice slightly different* from CBT. We are still developing the core mindfulness skills of concentration, sensory clarity, and equanimity as opposed to only positive thinking. The exercises we would use to do this are:

- Nurture Positive (generic)
- Nurture Positive (self-compassion)

Review of Part Three

Although it may seem like a lot at first, after you read over this step-by-step process and practice using it a couple of times, the two steps can soon become a natural way to regularly and strategically use mindfulness. Briefly, the general guidelines and two-step process are these:

1. General guidelines
   - Keep Body|Mind|World categories in mind
   - Awareness of turn toward/turn away strategies
   - Awareness of acceptance/change strategies
   - ION–choose a technique based on interest, opportunity, or necessity
   - Do what works

2. Two-Step selection process
   - What is the challenge focus?
     - difficult emotions or physical sensations (pain)
     - behavior change
     - stress
     - sense of self issues
     - personal development
   - Do you want to turn toward or away from the challenge at this time?
     - <u>Turn toward</u> to make *simple contact/track* and *deconstruct* sensations into manageable size by using the Focus on Body and Focus on Mind tools
     - <u>Turn away</u> and *deconstruct* using Easy Flow; or *ground* via relaxation with Easy Rest; or by *anchoring* with

Focus on World; or *reconstruct* with Nurture Positive. (Below is a chart summarizing turn toward/turn away options.)

Turn Toward	Turn Away
Simple Contact – Focus on Body, Focus on Mind, Both	**Grounding** – Easy Rest, Focus on World
Deconstruction – Focus on Body, Focus on Mind, Both	**Deconstruction** – Easy Flow
	Reconstruction – Nurture Positive

Part Four

Case Examples Using the Basic Mindfulness Toolkit

In this section we will look at several specific examples that demonstrate the application of the Basic Mindfulness Toolkit for the challenges presented in the last chapter. Some of the examples are students and some are from my psychotherapy practice. The cases will be presented based on the challenge identified as the focus of the mindfulness training. The format for each case will be:

- *Challenge*–the identified challenge focus for the exercise
- *Technique(s)*–what BMT technique was used in the exercise
- *Strategy*–the strategy used with the exercise on the challenge, e.g. deconstruction, simple contact, grounding, or reconstruction
- *Commentary*–a section that offers some of my thinking and other considerations when working with this particular challenge

In the course of these examples you get to know Kris, a client with whom I have worked for several years. Kris has, at one time or another, dealt with all the challenge foci using the BMT, and she will be presented for several of the challenge categories. This will offer a unique, in-depth look at one person and her integration of mindfulness over time.

Chapter Seven

Difficult Emotions and Body Sensations

JAMES HAS A SURPRISING REPONSE TO MINDFUL EXPERIMENTS WITH BODY AND MIND

I met James when he was a senior in college and wanted therapy for depression, anxiety, and relationship concerns. James was overweight in childhood and though now twenty-two and of a normal weight, he describes the experience of a "straight normal weight and a gay normal weight." A gay man, he feels most confident when he is twenty-five pounds thinner than he presently is. James has successfully used the Focus on Body, Focus on Mind tools with his anxiety many times and often takes notes on his cell phone to remind himself of insights.

James came to this session wanting help with his ruminations about his relationship with his boyfriend of the past year. James worried that when his boyfriend didn't want sex, it was a sign that he'd lost interest in the relationship. James "knew" intellectually that this was not likely but was "ruminating" (preoccupied mentally) about the relationship constantly. He claimed to "know everything there is to know about these feelings because I have them so often."

I suggested we experiment with some new ways to experience his ruminations that might help him accept/manage/understand their "feel" in the body. He was intrigued by the notion of experiments and enthusiastically agreed.

The first experiment I offered was something called "Noting X," which tracks the presence or absence of any sensation, "X," over time. I asked James simply to track whether or not rumination was present in his mind or body with the labels "zero" (absent), "subtle" (mildly present), or "strong" (noticeably present). I asked him to do this out loud rather than mentally. James liked the simplicity of just seeing if rumination was present or not.

After ten minutes we switched to another exercise called "Pendulating" in which, just like a pendulum on a clock goes back and forth repeatedly, we direct awareness back and forth between two contrasting sensations to gain insight from the contrast. Contrasts can be part versus whole (just the big toe versus the entire body), painful versus relaxed, mind versus body, and so forth. I had James compare the body versus mind components of his ruminations by slowly pendulating between them with the labels "Body" and "Mind." Within a few minutes James became teary so I stopped the exercise. He reported this: "As I followed the sensations back and forth in body and mind, really feeling them, I suddenly remembered myself when I was about ten or eleven, overweight, being teased, feeling alone and left out. I remember thinking then: 'If I just had the right body, my life would all be different.'" The rest of the session we discussed how James's felt sense of pain about his body was both the same and different when he was a child and now as an adult. By the end he was calm, no longer crying, and had taken many notes on his cell phone.

<u>Challenge/Techniques(s)/Strategy/Commentary:</u>

Challenge Focus: Difficult emotions
Technique: Focus on Body, Focus on Mind
Strategy: Turn toward the challenge; deconstruction into manageable size; simple contact/track change over time

Mindfulness is sometimes called "insight meditation," and James is a good example of how insights can naturally arise. The pendulation method in particular can produce this kind of result for several reasons. First, the fact that attention is specifically focused on some contrasting sensations, e.g. smaller area versus larger area, more intensity versus less intensity, mental components versus bodily components, invites the awareness of comparison. It demonstrates vividly that more than one thing is going on at the same time in the same bodymind.

Also, the fact that attention is moving means that awareness as a whole is moving as well. Movement is a form of Flow (change) and functions as a sort of purifier by breaking down fixations, cravings, aversions, and other physical, emotional, or mental events that block the natural flow of experience, sort of like how shaking out a towel or sheet expels the dirt or lint on it. Insight and Flow are intimately linked. When the natural flow of experience is not blocked in any way, the person has access to what Shinzen calls "the wisdom function"—that level of functioning in which the ego or self stops resisting or grasping particular sensations and relaxes into receiving whatever information is available in the entire Body|Mind|World continuum.

Insights from the wisdom function can feel like sudden flashes of memory, or a constant spontaneous flow of understanding without reflective or analytical thought. As with James, it often starts with simple things such as a psychological insight about our own behavior or the recognition of family patterns. This doesn't mean that perfect wisdom or even extraordinary wisdom is present. It is merely that a moment of insight into the nature of things has occurred. James had this kind of experience when he allowed himself to have a more complete experience of sensations in his entire bodymind personality.

LAURA LEARNS SOMETHING NEW ABOUT PERSISTENT PAIN

Laura contacted me to learn about mindfulness for pain. She started the conversation saying, "I have had migraines all my life; I need some new tools for dealing with them." Like many people with chronic pain, Laura has tried a number of medications, with varying success, to manage her recurring headaches. She can go up to a month without a headache, but they can also be severe for several days in a row. She is very motivated to find some other way to manage them because the headaches make her nauseated and light sensitive. As an artist, these symptoms can severely affect Laura's ability to make art, while the medications to help the pain can also make it impossible to work.

At first we simply did some education, because Laura did not know much about mindful awareness training. From working as an artist, she immediately picked up on the value of concentration and sensory clarity, but she didn't know the ways they could reduce both her physical pain and the emotional reactivity that creates the perception of suffering. Then we got to the practice part of our visit and Laura chose to lie on cushions on the floor for the training.

> *Janet: First, would you rate your pain right now as completely absent, subtle, or intense?*

> *Laura: I'm in a little pain from a bad headache a day ago, sort of the residue.*

> *Janet: Is the pain only in your head, or are other parts of the body uncomfortable because of the pain in your head? Sometimes head pain spreads to the neck or shoulders because of tension about the primary pain.*

Laura: The head is sort of achy but not intensely painful. And the back of one side of my neck is stiff and tense, sort of up into my head.

Janet: Okay, very good. It helps when you can detect things in such a precise way. We are going to practice focusing in that same, precise way both on the pain and away from the pain using restful states. Which would you prefer to start with: focusing on the pain or away from the pain?

Laura: Away from the pain.

Janet: Okay, get yourself into a comfortable position on the cushions. (JS gives some instruction on how to establish a meditative posture when lying down.) First we'll do some warm-up exercises. (Rings bell) Notice the body as a whole and what the body feels like physically as you are lying there. Just notice what it's like to be lying down. Now turn attention to your face. I'd like you to drop your jaw, let the jaw slacken, and notice the sensation of relaxation that occurs when you do that. Mentally note that sensation with the label "Feel Rest" every few seconds. You might be distracted by other sensations like sounds outside or thoughts in your head, or parts of your body that are not relaxed, and that's okay. Just let them be there, but turn your attention back to the jaw. Drop it again if you need to and note "Feel Rest" every few seconds.

(Janet leads Laura through warm-up exercise creating rest in the body and labeling it, then pointing out naturally occurring restful states in the body. Laura is taught to focus intently for a few seconds on the restful sensations and then allow attention to float broadly throughout the

body until another restful sensation occurs. Other sensations that distract her—mental talk, mental image, sounds outside, etc.—she is told to ignore without resisting.)

Janet: *(Rings bell to end session) First, can you tell me how well you were able to detect and pour awareness into the relaxed states we identified?*

Laura: *I really liked the restfulness in the breath. I felt like that was easy to contact. The rest in my jaw surprised me because I thought I could not relax anything around my head and having the front relaxed seemed to help the back some.*

Janet: *Can you tell me about your pain now? Is it worse, is it better, or is it just the same?*

Laura: *Well, the pain seemed better when we were doing the exercise. Now it is gradually returning, or maybe it never went away, but I was not as aware of it when we did the exercise.*

Janet: *Excellent! You are doing the technique exactly right if you can turn awareness away from the pain and onto something even slightly restful and presumably more pleasant. Now I'd like to add something to the technique of Feel Rest. (I went on to teach Laura to alternate between the pain in her head and the physical rest she had already contacted.)*

Laura: *That was really interesting. I never noticed that there were periods of relief even as the headache is going on. It also seemed that the pain sort of began to spread toward the other areas.*

Challenge/Techniques(s)/Strategy/Commentary:

Challenge Focus: Difficult emotions and physical sensations
Technique: Easy Rest (restricted to physical rest only); pendulate between relaxation and pain in the body
Strategy: Turn away with grounding via relaxation in body; turn away with deconstruction via flow

The example of Laura demonstrates two of the ways Basic Mindfulness works with physical pain. The first is finding and creating relaxation in her body. Anytime there is pain we usually find contraction of the body (tensing of muscles) and the mind (restriction of thought to just pain sensations). The second way of working with pain is pendulating between the pain and points of non-pain in the body. In Laura's case I had her pendulate between pain and relaxation and actually had her turn toward the pain in a new way.

As Laura's remarks show, even when we have a persistent pain condition there are ways to find something as pleasant as relaxation going on at the same time. Persistent pain has the impact of riveting our attention solely on "pain and finding relief from the pain." This can happen for so long that it seems as if pain is all there is. Or worse, *who* we are! Training yourself to *find or create* something restful in the body (no matter how much physical or emotional pain is also present) is a contribution of the Basic Mindfulness System.

The technique of pendulating to explore contrasts is used both in Basic Mindfulness and in body-based psychotherapy treatments such as Somatic Experiencing and the Hakomi Methods. This technique allows the client to touch the painful sensation but not be overwhelmed. This is actually an example of using flow because we emphasize the movement possibilities of all sensation by first moving our attention slowly back and forth. In doing so we are inviting the relaxation and pain to flow and spread out as well. Laura experienced the natural function of flow to help ease the discomfort by reducing fixation on it and allowing the pain to spread over a larger area.

ANCHORING IN THE OUTER WORLD TO CALM THE INNER WORLD

"I have anxiety issues. I'm afraid of elevators, airplanes, confined spaces in general. Oh, and I also get angry often, mostly at my ex-boyfriend who I broke up with two months ago. And I guess I should mention that I can be really picky. I need things to be 'just so' or I get upset pretty easy. Listen to me! It sounds like I have lots of emotions going on." This was Sandy's self-description when I first met her. Maybe you have felt the same way—many intense emotions pinging around, reactive thoughts, a sense of being overloaded.

Sandy and I worked together for many months to build up mindfulness skills to use with all of these different feelings and thoughts. She became skilled at noticing what triggered anxiety and often used Easy Rest to get calmer. Tracking body and mind helped her to disentangle intense emotions into smaller parts. She also participated in one of my group workshops in which I taught all the tools over six weeks. One day we were learning Focus on World (See Out, Hear Out) and Sandy came to the session late and flustered after learning her old boyfriend was dating someone she knew, and the person was pregnant. Sandy joined us to practice the Focus on World exercise and reported that she felt so completely distracted and drawn in by her inner thoughts and feelings that she was unable to focus at all on external sights and sounds. She pulled me aside and said she felt she should leave because she was so upset by her inner experience. Her internal sensations were so strong that she could barely tolerate being in the room. I encouraged her to stay so she could participate with the group in a walk that would help us Focus on World.

We got to a part of the program when we did an outdoor walking meditation to a nearby park, noting sights, sounds, and physical body sensations ("See Out," "Hear Out" plus "Feel Out"). Before we left she whispered to me, "I don't think I can do this. I'm just too upset, and I won't do it right." I told her, "Just do the technique, as you know it. If you do that then it's fine; it doesn't matter whether or not your feelings go away." Walking fairly slowly, the group took a long leisurely stroll, where there were trees, flowers, people playing with children, dogs, cars, smells, and sounds.

When we returned from the walking meditation, Sandy was the first to speak up:

> *"I can't believe it; it really changed me. I was totally in overwhelm. I 'knew' this wasn't going to help me because I couldn't concentrate. Then something got my attention outside, like a dog or a baby or something and I just looked at it and then I could look at something else. And then I tried to notice my feet and legs walking and just how that felt and then I heard a car drive by..... and then I got it...I got what you mean by 'anchoring' in external experience. So then I could keep doing it whenever a feeling or something inside would pull me away, I would just refocus on something outside. And by the time we were halfway through the walk I felt sooo much calmer."*

Challenge/Techniques(s)/Strategy/Commentary:

Challenge: Difficult emotions
Technique: Focus on World
Strategy: Turn away from the challenging emotions and ground in the sights, sounds, and physical sensations of the outer world.

Sandy's situation is an example of using external physical experience to "turn away" from painful interior thoughts and emotions. Her story sounds dramatic, but her experience is actually quite common. At first, people typically have trouble even putting attention anywhere but on the inner experience. Our inner life seems to *demand* that we give it constant and exclusive consideration. If you continue to label and hold attention over and over on the external world, eventually something interesting enough comes up to grab awareness externally and the inward pain drops away or diminishes significantly. Often it returns again very soon, but that one experience of relief produces important understanding. The period of practice time may differ, but there is often a sudden turning point in which the grip of interior experience is broken by the pull of the present moment, "The Power of Now (1)". Practicing the exercise may be slow, but recognition is sudden and usually powerful. In that significant moment we notice that the pain stopped. And perhaps it started up again as thoughts and emotions habitually arise and we attend to them once more, but now we know *consciously* what it's like to get away from the pain. It works the same as ordinary distraction, but because we do it systematically we train mindfulness *as well as* get relief.

KRIS LEARNS TO USE MINDFUL AWARENESS WITH TRAUMA

This case example may sound a little technical or medical because it's from my psychotherapy practice, and some may not relate to it. My client, Kris, and I have sorted through the impact of her childhood trauma for over ten years. Because of our long history together, she's had much practice using mindfulness for her symptoms. I use examples of Kris several times in this section, so I am including a little of her background.

Complex trauma can include a wide variety of physical and emotional symptoms that often seem unconnected to anything happening in the now. For this reason, people with this kind of trauma are not very present, i.e. they are not aware of what is happening now, in Body|-Mind|World. Kris experienced many of these states. She had odd face and body sensations, phobias, and depression. Her main coping strategy before therapy was to be a pleaser, the "good girl" she called it. We all need to be considerate and pay some attention to pleasing others, but as our only coping strategy it is very limited. Kris's only other options were to alternate between being "spaced-out" (we call that dissociation) or "ruminate" about details of some decision but getting nothing done. Over several years of work with me she has learned to use mindfulness and other treatments to reduce symptoms, recognize disowned feelings, be more present, and broaden her responses to more than these two.

One time Kris was telling me about an eruption of emotions based on a traumatic memory of being forced to go in the car with her diabetic father, who refused to manage his blood sugar and would drive erratically. She said her physical and emotional anxiety were so overwhelming, she would suddenly become incredibly sleepy while driving her own car. The urge to sleep frightened her even more.

As she was remembering this incident I asked her to close her eyes and start tracking individual mind and body components using "See In", "Hear In", "Feel In", "Feel Out" as labels. When she first noted sensations, she began to feel spacey (dissociate) and then wanted to talk more about the mental story of what was happening (ruminate). I suggested she narrow the scope to just her upper body. With gentle encouragement, she started making simple contact, tracking one component at a time. After a few minutes we stopped and she described the sensations: "buzzing in my cheek," "feeling like the left side of my face is moving," "mind says 'you are crazy; no one will like you if you do this.'" Gradually we expanded the tracking to her trunk and lower body.

Kris then became aware of intense anger sensations and realized they were toward her parents, especially her mother. I encouraged her to breathe deeply and continue to track mind and body. Finally, after about fifteen minutes, she blurted out, "Anger is easier than being scared! First I was anxious, but the anxiety was from my body feeling vulnerable and afraid in that situation and not being able to say, 'I WANT OUT OF THE CAR!'"

All these years, whenever she was in a car, Kris's body would remember suppressing what it was like to be that child in a frightening situation. Using the tracking tools of Basic Mindfulness, Kris was able to track backward from the sleepiness, to the anxiety, then fear, and finally anger.

Challenge/Techniques(s)/Strategy/Commentary:

Challenge Focus: Difficult emotions and body sensations
Technique: Focus on Body and Focus on Mind
Strategy: Turn toward, deconstruction of sensations into manageable size

Kris had a trauma memory in the session. Feeling the connection in the body at the same time we know it in the mind is a large piece of the trauma healing process. Mindful awareness, because it focuses on the present moment, is a key component of this healing. However, this kind of work may not be possible to do alone because of how overwhelming the feelings can be. Another person you trust, and often psychotherapy, are needed to provide proper support for experiencing and healing trauma. When your body feels that aroused, it needs another body that is calm and knows how to notice what is happening and downshift the arousal to a manageable level. Otherwise, the usual protective behaviors will kick in, i.e. in Kris's case, spacing out or ruminating.

Even though Kris wanted to escape the feelings triggered by spacing out and then ruminating aloud, I encouraged her to face her feelings (turn toward) by tracking them one at a time. Had it been a new client or less trusting relationship I would have either: 1) let her decide whether to turn toward or away and used Easy Rest or Focus on World to calm down; or 2) let her use her defensive habits again (dissociation, rumination) to down-regulate arousal even though they would not produce change. Remember that in therapy, we first want to avoid making things worse.

When Kris had the initial difficulty labeling, we narrowed the scope of her attention to only the upper body, also simply naming the sensation rather than labeling. You are free to keep narrowing the focus until you find a small enough bit of experience that is tolerable. This strategy of focusing on smaller and smaller units of experience is a key aspect of all Basic Mindfulness practices. Anyone can be successful facing painful sensations if they are dealt with in small enough doses. The result is a great feeling of empowerment; your body is no longer something to fear and avoid. How liberating!

Chapter Eight

Behavior Change

HELPING MARY CHANGE A LIFETIME OF IMPULSIVE SPEECH

Mary, a regular in a weekly mindfulness practice group I led, asked one day about using mindfulness with a lifelong problem she had: speaking impulsively when she was angry. She was going through a divorce, many contentious situations were arising, and she wanted to handle things differently.

First I gave everyone a little lesson about how the primary feelings of fear, panic, and rage are linked, and that her body was basically feeling in danger at those times she blurts things out. The problem is that the situations that cause the rage are not about being chased by a predator animal anymore; rather, they are modern-day threats to personal security and comfort, such as loss of resources, lack of esteem, unwanted changes in our living situation, and so on. When we feel threatened, we use facial gestures and a strong tone to "fight" and fend off the threat. With Mary this way of speaking had become exaggerated and habitual: she could not control it.

One way of changing this behavior is to train mindfulness to become sensitive sooner to the bodily clues that primary emotions are being triggered. Toward that end, I encouraged Mary to give extra attention to the Focus on Body exercises: to notice the subtle details of physical sensation that are precursors to the attacking speech and simply make contact and "be with" them.

Mary was a little disappointed because she had hoped for a quick solution and didn't understand how focusing on her body would stop her speaking the things she ruminated about in her mind. Nevertheless, she persevered and diligently practiced mindful awareness of the body for several weeks. Though she did have a few slips, fairly quickly Mary was able to notice and inhibit the urge to say angry things about her ex-husband to her children. Doing this with her ex-husband took much longer.

Several months later Mary said she was going to be meeting with her ex-husband to discuss property division. Beforehand we reviewed the pattern of mental images, mental talk plus physical and emotional responses caused by thoughts of speaking to him. She made a strong intention not to ask any unnecessary questions, but simply accomplish the task at hand while maintaining contact with her level of arousal. This time she was successful at changing her response to him even though she still *felt* the instantaneous anger.

Sometime later Mary came in announcing, "I did it! I'm so proud of myself!" She described an incident with her new boyfriend in which a difficult conversation began to stimulate the same feelings that would have resulted in a verbal attack on her former husband. She said, "I began to feel some shift in my body. I can't say exactly what it was but like tension and push at the same time, sort of. It felt different from when we started the conversation. At that moment I told my boyfriend, 'Let's stop the conversation for now,' and my boyfriend said, 'Yes, I don't think this (conversation) is productive right now.' We just changed the topic and the sensation faded away. But that is the first time I have been able to just *stop*, mid-conversation, and not react like I usually do. It felt *really* good!"

<u>Challenge/Techniques(s)/Strategy/Commentary:</u>

Challenge Focus: Behavior change
Technique: Focus on Body (Focus on Mind a little)
Strategy: Turn toward the challenge; deconstruction into manageable size; contact/track

In this example the use of deconstruction is to bring more **clarity and equanimity** to the body and mind sensations that trigger unwanted behavior. As you recall, mindfulness is composed of three skills: concentration, sensory clarity, and equanimity. When we develop the ability to quickly detect more and more subtle sensations, we are developing sensory clarity. When there is clarity, it is possible to bring conscious inhibition to reactions. The body has become conditioned to have an autonomic reaction to external triggers. If we can bring the noticing capacity to the subtlest cues that arousal has begun, it is possible for the mind to interrupt the reactivity generated in the body.

Mary practiced noticing her body long enough that she was sensitive to the earliest signs that she was getting negatively aroused. Her description of the sensations as "tension and push at the same time" is typical of this kind of subtle clarity. Unseen forces in the nervous system first become conscious as barely noticeable patterns of felt sensation that often have vague descriptions. Sometimes people will say, "I just sensed a shift" or "Something changed in my gut." This is a case in which invisible patterns of force become observable patterns of sensation(2). With improved sensory clarity, Mary detected these subtle patterns in her body, which allowed her to stop the progression to unwanted behaviors.

TURNING TOWARD FEELINGS PRODUCES INSIGHT FOR ELLA

Ella has the kind of busy life common to many modern women: a husband, two small children, and a demanding career. Her intensity shines from her face. Ella has a lot of physical and emotional troubles (body aches and pains, depression, anxiety, forgetfulness) and has worked on these issues using psychotherapy but called me to ask questions about mindfulness.

Ella's most pressing concern is conflict about her job and struggling to get herself to work. Several days a week she will take her kids to school and then go home and sleep for several hours. Obviously, her work product suffers and she is fearful she will be found out. I met with Ella and offered education about Basic Mindfulness and introduced the core techniques of focusing on body, mind, and world. She enjoyed these practices and felt like she was learning to pay much better attention to herself.

Then Ella came in one morning for a meditation session and was all caught up in worry about her parenting. "I nearly went back to bed and skipped this!" she blurted out, avoiding eye contact. I asked if she felt like experimenting with the worrying, to get to know the sensations going on there, and she agreed. We started by using Focus on Body. She noticed a small anxious sensation in the abdomen and wanted to talk about it in detail, so I prompted her to simply report location, intensity, and quality (if there was one). First, she reported a moderately intense quality in her abdomen she called "unsafe"; she continued noting and awhile later the same location felt more like the quality of "dissatisfaction."

Next, I instructed her to shift awareness to Focus on Mind (image and talk) and notice what happened in the body. She was surprised to discover that the physical sensations changed depending on what and how her mind thinks about things. If she has images of work, laborious tasks, or chores she doesn't enjoy, the body experience is dissatisfaction; if she has images of a memory from childhood, she feels unsafe. She could see that the felt sense in the body stayed the same, but her mind's interpretation would change the experience from one of feeling dissatisfaction to one of feeling unsafe. Once again, she wanted to talk *about* her experience rather than stay engaged *with* it, and I encouraged returning to simple contact with the mind-body sensations. This same cycle happened two or three times. Finally, she reported a memory of sitting outside alone, age three or four, having this feeling during a time of family stress (her father's affair), and moving her stomach muscles in and out. It soothed her to do this. Then Ella remembered many other kinds of body soothing tics she has that arose as she got older (nose twitch, lip curl, etc.). This lead to a conversation about mindfulness and self-soothing and she agreed to explore that together.

We tried several self-soothing activities (crossing arms and hugging; one hand on chest; one hand on abdomen, stroking upper arms) while she tracked the response from her body. Finally she said, "This is what would have felt good then." I asked her to continue tracking the body sensations while she comforted herself in these ways. After some minutes Ella was much calmer and said her eyes felt impossibly heavy; she had an overwhelming desire to lie down and sleep. With this we shifted to focusing on sights/sounds in the office, describing out loud the various details of what she saw. Ella admitted this turning to the world was extremely difficult. "I kept wanting to focus on my thoughts or the sleepiness, but I actually feel more alert right now."

Challenge/Techniques(s)/Strategy/Commentary:

Challenge: Difficult emotions and behavior change

Technique: Focus on Body, Focus on Mind, Soothe Body, then Focus on World

Strategy: Turn toward-(first); deconstruction using Focus on Mind and Focus on Body; turn away (second); grounding using soothing physical touch exercises and Focus on World

Ella is a good example of so many of us; she wants to talk "about" her feelings and sensations rather than experience them to see what information they have to offer her. Without practice, we often don't notice that physical and emotional sensations in the body have been immediately hijacked by the thinking process. This is a kind of mental defense to get away from the felt sense that is happening. Thinking is a process that creates, manipulates, and manages concepts and ideas. When we get relief from the actual feelings by "thinking about" feelings, thinking is reinforced as a way to manage them as well. Pretty soon we are in the habit of using "thinking about" as the best way to process anything. (Imagine processing our food with thoughts!) In fact, "thinking about" removes us from engagement and the "felt sense" of what is going on, which means we miss very important information.

Perhaps you recall a time when you asked someone how they felt about something and they responded with, "Well, I think it's..." Mind and body functions are both necessary. Feeling allows us to experience what is present; thinking, to reflect on it, consider solutions if necessary, and simply appreciate sensations we find in ourselves. Once Ella started feeling through her experience, she began to have insightful memories that resulted in sleepiness. We then used a Focus on World exercise to bring her to the vividness of *now*, counteract the sleepiness, and give her a more alert state of mind (her desired behavioral goal). Nevertheless, she reported a strong desire to return to sleepiness and think about things (both ways to avoid the felt sense of her life). This, too, is a pattern familiar to all of us—we avoid negative feelings about something and, over time, avoidance of feelings becomes an unconscious habit driving our behavior.

MAGGIE BEFRIENDS ALL OF HER THOUGHTS AND FEELINGS

Maggie had worked really hard to eliminate the narcotic medications that limited her productivity, interfered with her relationship with her family, and gave her only partial relief from trigeminal headaches. She found working with Rest and Flow were the most helpful mindfulness tools for her pain, and over time the physical dependency was gone. Maggie went on to re-engage with her family and finish and publish a book, and soon we moved her psychotherapy to every other week for maintenance.

On this day Maggie started the session with many entertaining stories about her kids and daily life events. From past experience I knew this was sometimes a way of avoiding issues that she didn't want to face. I asked her to talk about any feelings she might have about *not* wanting to come to her session that day. I encouraged her to be curious and address her divided feelings. In part she wanted to avoid the feeling of self-scrutiny; at the same time, she came voluntarily to her therapy session when she could have canceled.

As Maggie allowed *all* of her thoughts and feelings to be present, the "don't want to be here" part of herself spoke up and finally said, "Because I took some Vicodin last week and didn't want to talk about it." My response was, "Okay, let's not talk about why you took Vicodin and look at it in a different way. Are you having the impulse to take it now?" Maggie said it was always in the back of her mind as an option. "Would you be willing to experiment with looking closely at the sensations of 'wanting to take Vicodin'? What happens in the body and what happens in the mind when you have the desire to use the Vicodin? Can you detect in detail what the experience of that inner push is; what wanting (desire/craving) itself *feels* like? What, exactly, is the physical and psychological experience you want that is not present now?"

Maggie agreed to this experiment and we did a meditation to break things down so she could make contact with the components of her desire for narcotics. We explored what and where sensations happened in the body and mind, how these sensations changed over time, and how body and mind interacted with each other on this topic. As she focused I encouraged her to embrace each sensation in a friendly way and see what it had to offer. Here is what Maggie discovered about the urge to use the narcotics:

> *"At first I didn't feel anything in the body; the mind was saying critical things and distracting me. Then as you kept guiding me to stay in the body I noticed kind of a crying feeling in my eyes and throat and a feeling in my chest that I can only describe as 'want to get away.' It seemed like it would be relief from something, getting away from the pressure of having to be something, a mom, a wife, a writer, any responsibilities. The interesting thing is that it wasn't about headache pain at all, even though I am having moderate pain right now. I just want the mental/ emotional escape."*

Over the next several weeks Maggie reported trying this technique of using mindfulness to simply look at and accept the feelings or thoughts she had passively avoided or actively tried to push away. She found that when she let herself know more clearly the sensations that had formerly triggered her to crave and sometimes use narcotics, she became more able to use alternate ways of coping and reduce drug use. Though there are still occasional slips, Maggie now goes months, years, without abusing medications.

Challenge/Techniques(s)/Strategy/Commentary:

Challenge: Difficult emotions or physical pain
Technique: Focus on Body, Focus on Mind
Strategy: Turn toward the challenge with deconstruction into manageable size and accept unpleasant sensations as they are.

As we noted earlier in this book, a mindfulness approach values all sensation, even unpleasant ones, because it is part of what we are and carries information. When compulsive drug use is the challenging sensation, we would probably feel like Maggie and want to completely avoid the thoughts and feelings associated with it. It is not uncommon for us to do one of two things with most any pain—totally suppress the sensations or totally avoid all things that are associated with the behavior so it won't be triggered. With encouragement, Maggie allowed first her self-criticism and then the body sensations that were the triggers for her unintended drug use. "Making friends," so to speak, with the challenge itself is the first step of any behavior change. The belief that suppressing the feelings is helpful to changing behavior is based on the notion that "If it doesn't arise, I won't be tempted to act on it." The suppression strategy might work temporarily, but in the long run the sensations driving the behavior are pushed into the unconscious, where they simply influence the behavior outside of conscious awareness. Those who use the avoidance strategy are usually weary and ashamed of the behavior and get in the habit of instantly avoiding everything associated with the behavior, both external (people and situations) as well as internal (thoughts and feelings).

However, by slowly accepting things as they are—pleasant, unpleasant, or neutral—we begin to get the information we need to change behaviors. Sometimes we need a support group, sometimes it's training in certain types of self-soothing skills. But whatever it is, we cannot change something we don't allow ourselves to face and experience deeply.

USING THE PRESENT MOMENT TO REFORM THE PAST

A recurring theme in Kris's therapy was her goals around driving and generally traveling alone. When I met her, she was able to drive on her small town roads but could not travel faster than about 40 mph, and even then, if there were many other cars, she wouldn't take the chance. Although at one time in her life she drove easily on the freeway, her fears had increased gradually over time, reinforced by the primary relief of avoiding emotionally distressing situations. Kris wanted to change her present driving pattern and stop letting fear take over. To do that she would have to learn to both reduce and manage her fear: basically, change her relationship to fear.

In the course of our work together, Kris recognized that riding in a car triggered strong traumatic memories. Initially, she experienced numbness, derealization (the feeling of being not real in one's body), and the overwhelming sense that she might fall asleep and cause an accident. She remembered that falling asleep in the car was how she got away from her intense childhood fear of driving with her parents. We used Focus on World techniques to ground her in present moment reality, noting such things as "'These are my hands on the wheel," "I feel my foot on the pedal," "I see the road in front of me," "I see the trees on my right side," "I am driving safely now," "I can drive the speed that is comfortable for me." These practices helped her gradually increase her driving range and speed.

Then Kris came into a session and reported that she'd had an important experience while driving and wanted to explore it more fully. She said, "I was on a longer ride and noticed feelings like I had when I was a child with my parents. It was so strong I felt as if I *was* a child again. I could feel the 'child' feeling building up until I got overwhelmed and had to stop the car. What does this mean?" Even as she spoke of it she began to have the same reaction again. I told her it was a trauma memory triggering her nervous system at the autonomic (reflex) level and making driving impossible. I asked her to do a meditation exercise with me immediately using the feelings that were happening in the moment. "We want to notice the very earliest signal that the child part of you is present," I advised.

To explore her trauma memory for when the "child" appears I had Kris track body and mind slowly moment to moment, because the sense of self arises here. She wanted to stop several times and became really anxious. At first it was just discomfort in her face, lips, and mouth (feelings she would have as a child when she was afraid), but then she started having mental talk that was self-critical about how she was handling her fear feelings. "They said things like 'You should work harder not to be upset. You are not a child, just drive!'" Kris put her hands on her face and sobbed quietly. "I just had this surge of feeling in my body. I felt myself to be a shameful child, ashamed of even having the feelings I was having." We stopped the exercise until Kris composed herself.

When she felt calm again, Kris said, "I couldn't hear all of the talk, but I was clear on a few flavors of it. My mind tried to say: *'This isn't real'* but it **felt** so real that the words did not sink in." "What were the sensations that made it real for you, Kris?" I nudged gently. "It was the feelings in my body, all that tension in my body and face, but it didn't seem real until I had that wave of shame. The mental talk said: *'THIS is who you are, an anxious, shameful girl!'* and when it was combined with the actual emotion of shame, it became true."

"That was a very important insight for you, Kris…really let that sink in. Adding strong feelings to thoughts gives whatever is being experienced the sensation we call 'reality.' But today, in fact, you *are not* a shameful child, are you? Not now; not then. Then you were simply a scared child who didn't feel free to be afraid openly. Now you are an adult, re-experiencing your childhood feelings as a flashback, not as reality."

Before closing with Kris we went over what I had done and I processed with her how she felt about my pushing her a bit to continue feeling her trauma memories. This is an important step to take in working with traumatic memories.

Challenge/Techniques(s)/Strategy/Commentary:

Challenge: Behavior change (to expand her limited way of driving to be more fully able to drive whenever and wherever she wants)
Technique: Focus on Body
Strategy: Turn toward the challenging sensations of driving; notice impact on mental activity and sense of self

When we look at this session with Kris, we see that in fact it could have been put in any of the four categories of experience: difficult emotions and body sensations, stress, sense of self, or behavior change. This is because these four categories are not really separable; they are created to simplify and clarify ways to choose Basic Mindfulness tools. I chose behavior change because that is what Kris said she wanted to work on when the session started, i.e. she wanted to expand her ability to drive freely and had an experience she thought was important to making that change.

Essential to Kris in this session was the ability to recognize and manage trauma memories—thoughts and feelings that were being elicited by the nervous system in the present but which were based on threatening experiences in her childhood. The current understanding of trauma is that the nervous system learns to respond to danger at one point in time and then cannot distinguish real current threats from memories of prior threats.

Of significance here to therapists and clients alike is the fact that in this session we were treating trauma with mindfulness. Many therapists don't agree with using mindfulness for trauma; I think those therapists should not use it with their trauma clients. I find that I must be careful with it, but the act of noticing what is going on in the body and mind when there are trauma memories is crucial to helping the client relearn at the nervous system level that the trauma is in the past, that they are safe now. A great deal of evidence is available in the fields of somatic experiencing and neuroscience showing that mindfulness is a key psychotherapy tool for re-training the brain to see, hear, and feel that the present is very different from the past.

All this being said, *the decision to encourage Kris to experience her traumatic feelings was a clinical judgment I made in this case. It is offered here as an example of a particular way of using mindfulness in psychotherapy. My decision was based on a very trusting and long-term relationship with this client. It is not being recommended as the best decision in all cases, and is not the decision I might make with Kris under other circumstances.*

Chapter Nine

Stress

CORNELIA "NAILS" EASY REST

I met Cornelia not long after her father was diagnosed with ALS, Lou Gehrig's disease. She came from a family of activists; in addition to all of her father's treatment issues, Cornelia had been very busy with benefits, volunteering, fund-raising runs, and personal appearances for an ALS non-profit. Her overall stress concerning her father's condition and all that surrounded it was getting to her. She came to me because her primary care doctor suggested she explore mindfulness as a tool for managing stress. Cornelia is a former competitive gymnast and was already skilled at concentration and discipline.

We spoke for a while and I educated Cornelia on the possible use of mindfulness for her various concerns. Then I asked her which, out of all of her concerns, she would most like to work on at the moment. She said, "Mostly I need to learn to relax. I'm just tense all the time and my mind goes constantly. It won't stop even when I'm exhausted." We agreed to do the Easy Rest technique from the BMT.

I went through a long, slow meditation teaching the Easy Rest technique with an emphasis on relaxing the body first. When it was evident that she was in a moderately relaxed state, I introduced the visual rest component (grayscale blank behind the closed eyes) and allowed her mind to become absorbed in the blank visual screen. As a result of her former athletic training, Cornelia was a very quick learner. I could tell that she was deeply focused so I let her practice on her own for a few minutes, giving occasional prompts to educate and keep her on track. Afterward she said:

"I feel sooo relaxed. I never thought I could do that so quickly. My body kept feeling heavier and heavier and I started to get sleepy without trying. And it really helped that I had something to do with my mind. Whenever I started to have thoughts, I would just look at the blank in front of my eyes and concentrate there. I'm going to use this when I want to go to sleep!"

Challenge/Techniques(s)/Strategy/Commentary:

Challenge: Stress
Technique: Easy Rest
Strategy: Turn away from the challenge with grounding (rest)

Cornelia is one of those people who makes learning mindfulness look easy. Athletes have already "learned how to learn," for they have been given techniques to practice and know how to concentrate on them over and over. Also, sports incorporate a mental concentration component, whereas in many cases novice meditators have to first learn to build a degree of concentration. Building concentration means practicing until the student knows clearly the sensation of being "locked on" to the object of focus. In order to build concentration they have to have the motivation and discipline to practice regularly enough to develop the skill. For Cornelia, the ability to concentrate was already present because she had been taught to rehearse a perfect routine in her mind. Like mindfulness practices, mental rehearsal of the performance one desires actually changes the brain's neural patterns and increases the likelihood a perfect performance will occur.

RELAXING WITH THE BREATH

Amanda was adopted from Korea at the age of three (she is now thirty-five). Very quiet, she didn't often make eye contact from under her jet-black bangs. Amanda has a longstanding habit of worry, over-thinking, and hyper-self-criticalness about her social interactions as well as an autoimmune disease that seriously affects her lungs. These two together make Amanda self-conscious and over-focused on the body.

I asked Amanda if she wanted to learn more about using mindfulness for all the tension she carried in her body. She was open to exploring this, though she had tried to learn meditation a couple of times previously and found it unhelpful. After some education about mindfulness we agreed to use the Easy Rest tool to help her relax tension.

I decided to restrict the scope of the exercise to focus only on physical relaxation of the body. After I explained the noting technique we did a warm-up in which I showed her how to create relaxation in the body and then notice it (drop the jaw, drop the shoulders, clench and unclench fists). I guided her to note the parts that were already at rest—the outbreath, her hands in her lap, her left foot, and so on— and then instructed her to broadly float throughout the body noticing relaxed parts intently and ignoring distractions.

She slowly opened her eyes but stayed absorbed for several seconds, then said, "That was the best meditation experience I have ever had! Always before they had me control the length of the in and outbreath or try and slow it down in some way. My lung capacity is only forty percent of normal, and I either wasn't able to do it or it was distressing to pay so much attention to something that is a major source of concern. With this exercise I got so relaxed, even focusing on the outbreath was not a problem because we were just watching it."

<u>Challenge/Techniques(s)/Strategy/Commentary:</u>

Challenge: Stress (could also be seen as difficult emotions and body sensations)
Technique: Easy Rest
Strategy: Turn Away from the challenging mind and body tension to rest

Amanda has many physical and psychological stressors: a complex and traumatic personal history plus a chronic illness that both degrades her everyday existence and statistically is likely to shorten her life. To complicate matters more, she has actually tried to learn to meditate on the breath (body sensation) and found it only added to her distress. Given the focus on difficulties in her body, I thought it would be useful to offset this by helping find some rest and perhaps even pleasure in the body. Fortunately, Basic Mindfulness is different from most Vipassana (mindfulness) practices in that it purposely does not have breath practice as the primary anchor for attention. This allowed us to help Amanda focus on the body in a way that did not trigger the same painful arousal about breathing as prior meditations had.

The Easy Rest exercise is one of my personal favorites and has broad appeal with my clients, as well. There are at least two reasons for this: 1) It is very easy to learn, can be mastered quickly, and used in short bursts of a few minutes throughout the day; and 2) No matter what might be wrong with the body or mind, it invites a focus on what is pleasant in the body right now. Pain and illness very effectively demand our attention. The Easy Rest exercise gives us something else to focus on while still building mindfulness skills. We know from neuroplasticity research that mindful awareness exercises are experiences that compete in the brain for attention and thus weaken the brain habit of attending only to painful sensation (8) (9).

SURVIVOR'S GUILT AND NUTURE POSITIVE

Cornelia was a quick learner when it came to applying mindfulness to her symptoms. She used the Focus on Rest and focus on body and mind techniques independently and was pleased with her success. She was even teaching her mother and boyfriend how to use the exercises.

I didn't see Cornelia for several months and then she returned clearly depressed. Her life circumstances were good; her relationship with her boyfriend had deepened, she got a promotion at work, and her father was fairly stable. She reported stopping both her depression medication and meditation because she was feeling guilty. She said, "How can I be happy that my life is going so well and enjoy that when my mother and father are dealing every day with his illness?" She felt survivor's guilt about her own good fortune.

We talked about how to use mindfulness for the present situation. As we spoke about resources for self-soothing, she began to speak of her faith and the church she attends. I asked her if she had a favorite prayer or Bible passage she used when she was having a difficult time. Cornelia mentioned a "Thought for the Day" booklet that said something like: "God never gives us more than we can handle." So I suggested she do a meditation using that phrase in some way and she thought that would help.

Up to this point Cornelia had managed negative emotions by using Noting Body and Mind (deconstruction) or Rest within Body and Mind (grounding). Now was a good time to help her turn away from stress by supporting and nurturing positive feelings. I explained the basics of the Nurture Positive (NP) technique, and then we created some sentences that combined her need for permission to enjoy life and her Christian emphasis on grace. After experimenting with a few combinations we ended up with "May God grant me the grace to live and accept."

As she left our session, Cornelia said, "I already feel better. It sounds simple, but I'm alive, and my father is happy when I'm happy."

Challenge/Techniques(s)/Strategy/Commentary:

Challenge: Stress (persistent stress of terminally ill family member)
Technique: Nurture Positive, self-compassion version
Strategy: Reconstruct a positive self-cxperience by replacing negative mental talk with self-compassionate language.

If you have ever had to take care of someone with a chronic illness, you know that it is one of the most difficult stressors you will ever face. Over time your energy and emotional resources become depleted, yet the need for love, support, physical, and material assistance to the ill person continues. More is needed, but you either have no more to give or you just don't *feel* like giving anymore. Irrational thoughts and feelings can creep in, such as survivor's guilt. Cornelia felt guilty for being alive and happy while her father continued to decline. Over time this caused a stress reaction in Cornelia.

We could have proceeded to use the strategies of relaxation and deconstruction, but it seemed to me that Cornelia needed permission to feel good within herself. To do this she had to replace the negative thoughts (*How can I be happy when he is so sick?*) and feelings (guilt) with something more positive. This replacing of negative with positive is exactly the function of the Nurture Positive strategy. Cornelia already had positive words (prayer) that were familiar and comforting so combining them with the Nurture Positive technique was an ideal strategy to help her. Practicing this cemented a more rational and adaptive attitude for Cornelia as she faced her father's ongoing, inevitable decline.

USING MINDFUL AWARENESS TO STRENGTHEN PERSONAL BOUNDARIES

Kris often mentioned having trouble maintaining her own boundaries and perspective when she was either under stress or felt interpersonal pressure to listen and agree with someone else. For example, when she stood on the sidelines watching school sporting events with other parents, she would find herself compulsively forced to participate in conversation and attentive listening even when she preferred being focused on the game. Similarly, if someone called on the phone wanting a lengthy talk about distressing personal news, she felt helpless to end the conversation. Kris would compliantly listen as long as the other person wanted to speak, gradually feeling more negative emotions as she took on their distress. By the end of these kinds of stressful encounters she would feel exhausted and unable to take care of her other responsibilities.

In session we practiced how to stay in contact with her own needs by tracking her mind and body and really isolating them as hers (e.g. "**this** feeling is in **my** body, **that** feeling is **her** feeling; **this** is **my** mental talk, **that** is **her** mental talk, etc."). We would use recent experiences or role-plays to get a lot of present time practice. After some period of practicing this technique Kris was excited to report how she had used her mindfulness skills:

> *"I had two situations happen that I wanted you to know about where I was able to track what was going on for me **during** the conversations and it felt so different. Both were about medical things, which always seem to trigger me. The first one was when I had a call from the doctor about a possible problem with a Pap smear. At first my body felt a little frozen, then I could hear worrisome mental talk, BUT I WAS ABLE TO TRACK IT! and still*

listen to the doctor. Everything turned out to be okay and I was so proud that I hadn't let the stress of her words get me upset. Later that same day my sister-in-law with lung cancer called with news that they found new spots on her brain. Again, I just tracked what was happening to me as I listened and responded to my sister-in-law. I felt concerned but not overwhelmed and could be supportive.

I didn't really realize how well I had done until I spoke to my daughter the next day. She told me that she was so upset speaking to her aunt that she cried all night and her body was shaking uncontrollably. She does not have mindfulness tools. I could have gotten upset as I heard my daughter being so upset. My mental talk actually said, 'You are numb. Something is wrong with you.' But I noticed that I did feel concern for my daughter and sister-in-law and was not numb. I was being mindful! I realized what life with mindfulness really is and I felt like I could handle anything!"

Challenge/Techniques(s)/Strategy/Commentary:

Challenge: Stress (pattern of arousal when listening to the personal distress of others)

Technique: Focus on Body and Mind

Strategy: Turn toward the challenge (differentiating her own thoughts and emotions from those of others in a stressful context). Deconstruct her own thoughts and feelings and be able to know clearly what her own feelings were and what belonged to the other person.

Though we may not always feel so trapped by the strength of feelings in another person, I think we can all relate to Kris's experience. The key to using mindfulness in interpersonal situations is the ability to have what we call dual awareness—awareness of thoughts and emotions in ourselves as well as the thoughts and emotions in the other person—without getting confused or overwhelmed. The challenge is that we are vulnerable to falling into both extremes: either becoming fused with the other person's thoughts and feelings as if they were our own (identification), or disengaging by dissociating (consciously or unconsciously splitting theses sensations off from awareness). For someone with a trauma history this challenge can be much more of a struggle.

Kris's mindfulness practice helped her develop the skill of making contact with her own thoughts and feelings *and* know they were her own, as well as making contact with the caller's thoughts and feelings *and* know that they belonged to the other person. We can hear in her voice the sense of empowerment she felt being able to do this. If you recall, earlier in this book I mentioned an equation that Shinzen offers regarding suffering versus empowerment. With this example of Kris it may make more sense so I offer it again here:

SUFFERING = PAIN **x** RESISTANCE

EMPOWERMENT = PAIN **x** EQUANIMITY

Chapter Ten

The Sense of Self

AMANDA REPLACES HER INNER CRITIC WITH COMPASSION

A quick web search of the term "self-criticism" yields a flood of articles, blogs, and books about the topic. A significant number of us have this habit of saying hostile things to ourselves. The range and quality of the criticism can be mild ranging from: "You could have been more tactful" to vicious: "You are worthless and can't do anything right. You should just kill yourself!" People tell me they're afraid they won't be motivated or try hard enough without it, but in fact it does not help us accomplish our goals. It causes negative emotions like shame, embarrassment, and disappointment, and because our sense of self includes emotions, *we begin to feel like we are shameful, embarrassing, disappointing people.*

Amanda's inner dialogue has been negative for as long as she can remember. "It's just how I think to myself. Doesn't everyone do this?" she asked me one day. Her habit started in childhood as a protective mechanism and is very connected to her sense of self, i.e. it's "who" she is. She thought if she was perfect, she could avoid her mother's anger and violence. Now, she sees herself as "a person who" must constantly monitor and control her emotions and behavior; it's part of her identity. The fact that it is not sustainable *and* it doesn't help her accomplish her goals is incomprehensible to her. So what do we do?

We might suggest just stopping this behavior, like you would stop tapping your foot. But are *you* able to predict what your next thought will be? I'm not. Trying to stop certain thoughts from coming but allowing others would be futile for me. Some psychotherapies encourage shouting *Stop!* to yourself mentally whenever a critical thought arises. People tell me this does stop things momentarily, but to me it feels kind of like I'm yelling at myself, which feels just as bad as the self-criticism.

The Basic Mindfulness approach is not to fight with the negative thoughts but proactively think more constructive ones and ultimately *replace* the negative contents with neutral or positive contents. As you know by now, this process is called Nurture Positive in the Basic Mindfulness System. In practice, however, the procedure often generates very negative thoughts and feelings when first used due to that negativity bias that we discussed in Part Three. The negative habit gets started easily and will reassert itself strongly when change is introduced. So we want to be accepting of the paradox that saying positive things to ourselves might feel mistaken, uncomfortable, or unacceptable at first.

Thus I proceeded to gently suggest to Amanda that she try another, very different kind of meditation. After explaining the Nurture Positive concept and the procedure of self-compassion (including the warning that it might trigger fear and naysaying from the sense of self that was committed to protection), I led her in the following series of self-compassion themes:

May I have compassion for myself

May I be kind to myself

May I be free of suffering

May I be filled with physical health and vitality

May I have inner peace and contentment

May I have clarity and wisdom

May I live in love and harmony

She was instructed to simply say each sentence in her mind and then notice the sensations in the body. If the body response was positive, she was to try and sustain that response; if the response was neutral or negative, that was okay, too: she was to observe it with equanimity. If she had distracting mental images or mental talk, she was to simply leave those in the background of awareness. Each sentence could be repeated a couple of times in the mind. At the end of the exercise, Amanda said this:

> *"At first I could hear my mind telling me this should not be for me. I should offer it to others first, but your prompt helped me to leave that alone and gradually I could focus on just the sentence and some positive feelings that it triggered. I was surprised that I could feel a pleasant feeling even with the negative going on behind."*

Challenge/Techniques(s)/Strategy/Commentary:

Challenge: Sense of self
Technique: Nurture Positive
Strategy: Turn away from distorted cognitions about herself and replace them with themes of self-care and self-compassion (reconstruction).

Amanda will have to practice this exercise over and over to first soften and then replace the cognitive distortions about her sense of self. As mentioned earlier, for many people the initial expression of positives toward ourselves seems to elicit exactly the opposite. For most people, the negative reactivity is broken through after a few repetitions of the exercise.

For those of you who have deep-seated self-hatred, and deep faith in the protective power of self-negation, please go slowly and gently introducing the Nurture Positive technique. It is capable of producing profound change. If you find that introducing positive statements is too threatening, start by simply saying the words "calm," "compassion," "ease," "joy," without the "May I be/feel" part at the beginning. You might also think about all the ways that self-negation has been valuable to you. That belief system, even an irrational one, may have served you at some point and it's okay to acknowledge that importance while considering other beliefs that may serve you better now.

RITA OPENS THE DOOR TO A NEW SELF

When we met, Rita said, "I like to think of myself as a strong person so it was really hard to admit I had a panic attack," and then later, "I have always been a person who *cannot* disappoint anyone, even if it means I have to make all the sacrifices."

Whenever I hear someone introduce themselves with words like: "I'm the kind of person who…," I know that at some level they believe their identity, the sense of self, is fixed and does not change. Then something comes along that totally contradicts who they thought they were and stress symptoms begin. Rita had several work and family stressors that made it impossible to be "strong" or "pleasing." Her panic was actually a warning signal that she had emotional limits. Like many people, Rita had the idea she was always "strong" and "pleasing," so it took some serious panic symptoms and inability to work to get her attention.

There are a lot of BMT tools we could use to deal with Rita's situation. We could focus on the difficult emotions directly and bring deconstruction of the anxious elements (Image, Talk, and Feel) by simply noting them one by one with acceptance (Turn Toward/Be With). We could also teach her to relax using Easy Rest or Focus on Relax in the physical body. This would bring calm to the physical and emotional aspects of her anxiety (Turn Away/Grounding).

Finally, we could work with Rita's sense of self, which has cognitive (mind) distortions or mistaken beliefs. Rita was quiet and mild-mannered and learned to be rewarded for being the "quiet, shy, and good" one. Later, she came to misunderstand herself as *worthy only when being of service to others* and pleasing them. From these and other misunderstandings (mental component) Rita developed a self-sense that included being unattractive, uninteresting, and having little to offer in relationships except her ability to give people what they wanted. The emotional (body) components of her sense of self came to be feelings of insecurity, unworthiness, and reduced drive to explore and play.

In most cases I start people off by making contact with body and mind sensations, but when Rita asked to do something that might "feel good right now," I suggested Nurture Positive. This would both be a soothing feeling (body sensation) and begin to replace her distorted thoughts (mind sensations) with more positive and accurate ones. I taught her the self-compassion version of the nurture positive technique. This practice forced her to give herself the same attention and care she so effortlessly gave others. She cried at first when we went over the affirmations: "May I be kind to myself," "May I be happy," "May I be at ease," and so forth. But soon she said, "I really should give myself a break, shouldn't I? I like how you say it was just a misunderstanding that I believed I wasn't worth as much as my sister or anyone else. It feels not so permanent."

From here on things only got better for Rita. Her first action was to request that some of her duties at work be reassigned, rather than face the expectation that she work as many hours as needed to get the job of several people done. Next she set a limit with her grown children about how often they could leave the grandchildren with her on weekends. Then she set a goal to do something just for herself each week, such as a manicure, a massage, or a coffee date with a friend. These changes coupled with other skills for preventing panic attacks reduced her stress and improved her mood and self-image.

Challenge/Techniques(s)/Function/Commentary:

Challenge: Sense of self
Technique: Nurture Positive (Self-Compassion version)
Function: Turn away from the mistaken understanding and reconstruction with an attitude of self-compassion.

When I think of Rita, I am reminded of how important it is to really ask honestly: Do you want to turn toward or away from the present challenge? Especially in my role as a psychotherapist, people want me to give them professional advice, tell them what is best for them. However, sometimes the best advice is: "Check in with your own body and mind; see if you can sense what is best for you right now."

Rita, in particular, got her sense of value from pleasing others, getting it right in their eyes. We all feel this way to some degree, don't we? If we are hosting company, we watch responses to see if we "got it right" with food and atmosphere. If we are students, we want to get good grades from the teacher. For Rita, getting it right included being the "best therapy client" for me. Even though my initial thought was to suggest she learn to make contact with body and mind sensations, when she hinted that she would like to do something to feel better *now*, it immediately caught my attention: she was actually asking for something to please herself!

When I agreed to do something that was likely to feel good right then, the look on her face was like that of a kid who had just been let out of school. Eyes brightening, she inquired, "Really? It isn't avoiding the hard work to focus on something that feels good?" "No," I replied. "It isn't avoiding when you set the intention to turn away using concentration, clarity, and equanimity *and* are willing to turn toward the challenging experience at some point." This was Rita's first lesson in self-care and being respected for asking directly for what she really wanted.

TRACKING THE EVER-CHANGING SENSE OF SELF

I worked with Kris for many years to help her heal traumatic responses and learn new behaviors. Part of this was learning to incorporate new experiences and behaviors into her sense of self and expand it to have more options for living her life. For example, she got divorced and had to learn to do many things independently, like take care of a house, handle finances, do small repairs and maintenance, drive a car, relate to her children as a separate adult, and so on.

Trauma had long kept Kris stuck in an immature sense of self, but her experience applies to all of us. The river called Life is relentlessly moving, changing, turning, and demanding that we let go of past expectations, accept new conditions, try out new behaviors, and flow with it. At times we may feel like we are drowning; however, the alternative is to resist changing as Life changes, which produces more suffering. The tools in the BMT are designed to help us get in touch with the ever-changing self and relax comfortably into the adaptations required of us as we join the flow of that river.

One time Kris was describing the decision she had made to sell a sailboat. People's calls about the boat triggered many different feelings and with each new feeling a new "self" seemed to arise. For example, at first she felt like she was a "miser'" for selling the boat and wanting money instead of saving it for her children to enjoy. Next she felt foolish because she had no idea how much money to ask for, nor how to negotiate with potential buyers. Then she felt like a young "pleaser-good-girl" when speaking to someone who called about it. Finally, she felt dishonest when she didn't volunteer that there was a minor leak in the boat when the buyer didn't ask about its condition.

As she described the rapidly changing inner experience of miser, fool, good girl, dishonest seller, she quickly became confused and upset. I reflected to her that she seemed to be experiencing several motivations related to selling the boat; she wanted 1) to get it out of her driveway; 2) money; 3) to be a good girl; 4) to be a savvy adult conducting a business transaction; 5) not to talk about the leak unless the buyer asked; 6) to feel like she was an honest person. Each motivation was like a different "self." I asked her if she would like to do a ten-minute experiment in which she tracked the different selves as they floated into awareness. She immediately agreed to this.

Afterward, Kris reported feeling calmer and clearer. "I can see clearly for the first time that there are lots of different 'me's' and that I'm changing all the time. The young 'me' worked so hard to be perfect and control things so that they would never change, so that I would never change. That control is breaking down and it was scary for me at first, but mindfulness gives me a way to watch things from a safe distance."

Challenge/Techniques(s)/Function/Commentary:

Challenge: Sense of self
Technique: Focus on Mind and Body
Function: Turn toward with simple contact; use special labels to identify and make contact with felt-sense of self.

Earlier in this section I described some of the ways that the sense of self can run into problems of being too tight, too loose, distorted, or lacking integration. As with many trauma survivors, Kris is an example of someone whose "self" was initially too tightly organized around ways to protect herself and be safe, like being a "good girl" and "pleaser" to avoid alienating caregivers or attachment figures.

This required suppressing her own needs and motivations as well as negative thoughts and emotions, resulting in multiple physical and emotional symptoms. In the course of treatment Kris began to loosen her too-tight and childlike sense of self and assemble a more adult self of being in the world. This particular session shows her having conscious experience of multiple motivations and feelings, which is dramatically more flexible than when she started therapy.

Kris's experience is a good example of the confusion and overwhelm people experience with rapidly shifting mental and emotional states before they are taught how to track them. Two critical skills helped her to reduce distress:

1. The mindful ability to observe experience rather than be fused with it; and
2. Having experience with the distinct sensations that combine to create the sense of self. Using these two skills, Kris was able to identify and accept that she could be many selves, not just one fixed and self-protective one. We see her in the session moving from reacting to multiple thoughts, feelings, and body sensations to a calmer recognition of the various "selves" she is capable of being.

While trauma survivors are typically warned to be careful about using meditative practices because they can re-trigger traumatic memories, it is also true that mindfulness skills (being clear and in the present rather than past or future) are in fact what their recovery is all about.

FLOWING ON A RIVER CALLED LIFE

In the previous story, Kris was tracking the specific mind and body sensations that make up the momentary sense of self, an "I" (subject) that is experiencing the flowing river called Life (object) in a particular way. It is also possible to experience the world from just the flow standpoint, not as a subject noticing an object, but simply being in the flow itself. Here is Kris a week or so after the last example.

After discovering that she had many kinds of "me's" that would cycle through, Kris returned and wanted to do more work with the sense of self as it changed from one flavor of "me" to another. Because she had experienced a lot of intense emotions the prior week, I suggested that she use a version of the Easy Flow technique so that her attention was on background movement and evolution of her feelings rather than the fixed experience "I am a scared child" or any other particular "self."

The traditional Easy Flow technique focuses on the expansion/contraction, change, movement, and energy qualities of the breath (chest area). Kris reported feeling most of her emotions in the face and chest so we added the face to the areas of focus. First, she noted any "Body" sensations ("Feel In," "Feel Out") to see what sense of self was present, and then switched to "See Flow, Feel Flow" in just the chest and face areas of the body. This is like changing your attention from the specific details of physical and emotional to softer awareness of the background movement contours of these sensations. It is deconstructive in that the fixed thingness is reduced, like noticing the wave movement in a field of wheat. The field of individual stems appears to be more like flowing liquid than individual plants or heads or seeds of wheat. After about fifteen minutes, I had Kris wind down by ceasing all labeling and noticing the sitting still body.

When she opened her eyes, Kris stared for a moment and then said, "That was so interesting. When I switched to noting flow in the face and chest, there was a sense of immediate relaxation, like I was just floating in a river with what was happening. It didn't matter what it was. Then I would go back to noting "Feel In" and "Feel Out" as well as "See I" when images of myself arose. It seemed easier to be aware of the child self and the adult self without so much reaction after doing the floating."

We talked some more about the exercise and what her "child" sense of self felt and looked like versus her "adult." I asked her, "What did you discover makes you feel most adult? What did you look like? What were you doing?" Kris realized that she felt most adult when she did things like speak on the phone to her children (in the role of parent), wear earrings, do responsible-type activities like clean the garage. We used this information to help prompt the arising of the "adult" when it felt like her "child" was too much present. The result was that Kris felt empowered and effective, less at the mercy of triggered emotions.

Challenge/Techniques(s)/Function/Commentary:

Challenge: Sense of self, managing the "adult" versus "child" selves.
Technique: Focus on Body and then Easy Flow
Function: Turn toward the self-sense challenge first with simple contact, then deconstructing it into flow by focusing on some challenging sensations, noticing background movement/change qualities.

Kris experienced how you can learn to notice your experience at several different levels *and* the usefulness of being able to move between these levels. At first Kris could only report odd symptoms of muscular tension/tingling in her face and chest. Over time and with mindfulness training, she tracked her challenging sensations and saw that they were body/mind reactions to childhood events (body flashbacks, so to speak). She had the insight that these sensations had become combined and conditioned to produce a "frightened and helpless child" sense of self that felt like a reality in present time.

In this session, with a different mindfulness tool, Easy Flow, Kris experienced those *same sensations* as merely a river of vibration, not as a "scared child." They are exactly the same sensations that resulted in anxiety, fear, and a "child" self, but now she encountered them as a flow of energy and could tolerate them enough to learn from them. Kris's experience is not unique. With practice anyone can learn to tolerate difficult thoughts and feelings, either as individual strands of sensation, or from the Flow standpoint, relaxed in a river of movement.

Part Five

Where Do I Go From Here?

Toward the end of meditation retreats there is customarily a talk about how to integrate what has been learned into the general movement of Life. How often to practice the exercises, how much time to spend on each one, and where to go to practice with other people who meditate are some typical questions. This final chapter will cover some of these questions and suggest resources for others.

Chapter Eleven

Establishing a Routine; Finding Support

MAINTAIN THE INTENTION TO PRACTICE EVERY DAY

Setting the intention every day to have a daily practice routine helps to make that happen. Even on the days that I end up not meditating, I get up with the full intention of doing so that day. It makes a difference, like something has been "turned on" in my brain, and I have more ability to "just do it," as they say at Nike.

I have meditated for over thirty years and it took me fifteen of them to come to the place where I meditated every day. Before that I would start and stop. My life circumstances were usually the determining factor. When things were going badly (i.e. I was suffering more), it was easy to pour myself into a contemplative focus because it made me feel better. When life improved, it was easy to stop because I wasn't feeling badly. As I matured, I began to realize that old age, sickness, and death will come to everyone, including me. And by the time we are old and sick it is extremely difficult to bring one's attention to learning a new skill. "Waste no time," says the Buddha. "Strive diligently."

FIND YOUR PLACE AND SITTING TIME

It also helps to have a time of day and place that you can incorporate into a daily routine for yourself. Some people jump out of bed and want to do it right then. There are many advantages to this. Our

157

surroundings are usually quieter and we are personally quieter early in the morning because there has been a period of calm and restoration while we sleep. This is also a time when we might be able to be up before kids and others need our attention.

But not everyone is an early bird, so for some, evening is better. Others find a quiet moment during a lunch break at work, or take a walk outside and sit focusing on their external environment. Still others prefer to find a group to sit with rather than sit alone. Buddhist meditation centers and monasteries typically have early morning and evening drop-in meditation times in which the public can attend as part of the community.

SMALL EFFORT, MANY TIMES

One frequent misunderstanding about mindfulness and training mindful awareness is that it's not worth doing unless you can devote hours of daily practice. This is completely false. From a neuroscience perspective what we are trying to do is use mindfulness to rewire our brains. Each time we concentrate attention on particular events we are encouraging those neural networks in the brain to get stronger. We are rewiring the habit of attention. For "rewiring" to happen we need many repetitions of intensity, rather than one big moment of "change my brain!"

The good news here is that short but more frequent bursts of activity can make significant change over time. Taking about three minutes several times a day to notice clearly and with strong intention, "What is happening in my body? What is happening in my mind? What is happening in my world?" is just such a burst of rewiring activity.

When I was studying with Thich Nhat Hanh, he would do the same thing by having us stop and notice our breath while we were doing ordinary things that happened often during the day, such as when the phone (or any bell) rang, when we changed from one position to another (e.g. sitting to standing, standing to walking), when we went to wash our hands, while cutting the vegetables. The point is the same: getting in the habit of paying attention in a new way. Habits change as we practice new behaviors over and over. Mindful awareness is the same.

Pick a few exercises or bits of exercises and set the intention to do them as often as you can. This practice of small effort, many repetitions will go a long way to deepening your mindful awareness. To learn more about small daily practices you can also explore "Just One Thing" at Rick Hanson's website: https://www.rickhanson.net/writings/just-one-thing/

LONGER PERIODS OF MEDITATION

In the beginning our goal is to meditate for ten minutes on most days. Gradually, however, we sit for longer and longer periods to allow mindful awareness to grow deeper and more stable. When I lived in Vermont, Thich Nhat Hanh opened the Green Mountain Dharma Center nearby. They would offer "mindfulness days" in which the community would come and participate in sitting, walking, and eating meditation for an entire day. I found the extended practice time to be key in my development of a strong, daily meditation habit. Other opportunities for longer periods are residential retreats that offer between three days and three months of continuous practice. Here are some meditation centers that offer complete programs of mindfulness training and practice:

Insight Meditation Society, Barre, MA

Cambridge Insight Meditation Center, Cambridge, MA

Spirit Rock Meditation Center, Woodacre, CA
Insight Meditation Center, Redwood City, CA
*Cloud Mountain Retreat Center, Castle Rock, WA

If you look in the back of magazines like *Lion's Roar*, *Buddhadharma*, and *Tricycle*, you can find practice programs, practice groups, and retreat centers listed by geographical location. A quick web search can also bring up additional international options.

In the References and Notes page for Part V there are citations for my website, Shinzen Young's website plus some resources for web-based instruction and support.

This center offers retreats featuring teachers from all of these meditation training centers. It is not affiliated with a particular Buddhist tradition.

Chapter Twelve

FAQs

1. How often and how long should I meditate?

We have compared mindfulness to a gym workout and physical exercise. It seems to work best with mindfulness exercise to start small in scope of practice and length of time. So, take just one exercise, or even part of one exercise (e.g. just physicality, just emotions, just external sounds, etc.) and spend ten minutes a day on it. If you find yourself naturally wanting to meditate longer, that is fine.

As I mentioned earlier in this section, challenging yourself to sit for longer and longer periods of time is a natural way to grow and deepen your mindful awareness practice.

2. I feel like I'm distracted for nearly the whole time I meditate. Am I wasting my time?

No, you are absolutely **not** wasting your time. Your intention and willingness to sit and struggle to get *concentrated* is what meditation looks like at this point. At deeper levels your mind and brain are picking up on the fact that you are intending and giving a lot of attention to learning this new skill and in time you will pick it up. If it is of any comfort, even very seasoned meditators still have days when it is difficult to concentrate.

3. I find myself distracted by trying to label. Should I just stop?

The complete answer is both yes and no. Noting or "noticing" is the main activity of insight meditation and so is not optional; however, labeling what we are noting is optional. So in one sense, the answer is "Yes, it is okay not to label." Many students start out labeling all the time and gradually drop it unless it is really necessary.

On the other hand, labeling itself is a sub-skill and it can take practice to get the hang of it. People often report wrestling with it at first, even experienced meditators. In time it is completely effortless and mostly invisible.

The reason to keep labeling until you become skillful with it is that it can be a very useful tool to have in your toolkit even when you don't use it all the time. In addition to clarifying sensations, labeling is help-ful when you are experiencing extreme circumstances (overwhelm), have been hijacked by emotions, are very spacey, or are falling asleep.

4. Sometimes I forget to label, or am late labeling, or things are going by so fast I can't label them all.

Basic Mindfulness has something called "The 4 OKAY's" with respect to labeling. They are:
- It's okay to be late (especially at the beginning and for just a few seconds).
- It's okay to miss some things (you don't have to label everything).
- It's okay to guess (don't agonize, just guess and move on to the next event).
- It's okay to aggregate (such as when visual images flit by quickly).

The general idea is that you don't work so hard to get labeling "right" that you lose contact with what you are noticing.

5. *When a teacher leads the meditation exercise, I am able to have a more concentrated experience than when I do it on my own. Is this a problem?*

First, I would like to suggest you view what happens or doesn't happen in a meditation exercise with curiosity rather than as a "problem." Like "Oh, this is interesting. My mind is really scattered today." It is simply what is happening now. What happens *now* is the natural outcome of many causes and conditions, e.g. how long you have practiced, how you are feeling at the moment, the support you are getting in your life at this time, the current weather, what you ate or didn't eat today, whether your bladder is full or empty, and so on. It's all just what is going on in the natural flow of life, not a problem. And whatever it is, it will change over time.

Generally, with regular practice, things progress on their own in the direction of more CCE: concentration, sensory clarity, and equanimity. If, after a reasonable period of time, it feels like things have not progressed for you at all, then it is time to talk to a teacher/facilitator personally about what is going on. They will ask more questions and be able to offer some advice for your particular situation.

6. *I feel like no matter what position I try, I cannot get comfortable. I keep moving and fidgeting and adjusting my posture but nothing works.*

Getting comfortable in a posture is almost always a challenge when we first start meditating and can be challenging from time to time over the course of a practice life. Sometimes it's because we need to try out different postures to see what works best or change posture due to injury or aging. I sat cross-legged for years and found it very stable and supportive to concentration. But then I developed a nerve problem in one foot and had to change posture altogether to a kneeling position. It took a period to make this new posture "my own," so to speak.

It is not entirely natural to sit still for as long as this practice requires. Things get stiff when we are not moving regularly, and the body doesn't like discomfort, even when it is natural (e.g. after normal inactivity, like sleep, we move slowly and stretch ourselves out from that period of physical stillness). Most of the time we are unconsciously shifting and adjusting our bodies to renew our comfort level and when we decide to meditate, we are interrupting that unconscious adjusting process.

Part of the learning in meditation is to notice body discomfort and not do anything about it except relax into it. See what happens when you do that: notice the discomfort in detail and relax around it. After practicing non-reaction (i.e. not adjusting and moving) to the discomfort it's like the body learns that "this is going to be the way it is for now" and relaxes more automatically, stops fighting and tensing. It also means that you are not as controlled by what the body wants.

7. My mind just keeps thinking, thinking, thinking. I can't make it get quiet.

There is no instruction in this book that says you need to "make your mind quiet." That is one of the many misunderstandings about what mindful awareness practice is.

It *may happen* that as a result of practice that your mind becomes quieter, and if so enjoy that. But we are not in charge of making thoughts happen and we cannot automatically make them stop. We *can* stop paying attention to thoughts, leave them in the background of awareness, and not fight with them. In Basic Mindfulness this is called "background equanimity" and it is one of the skills we seek to cultivate. When we practice non-interference with any sensation, it is free to come, go, flow, increase, decrease, or vanish in whatever way life intended for it.

8. In another system I noticed I practiced more and went deeper when someone would lead me in an exercise. Are there recordings available for the Basic Mindfulness Toolkit exercises?

Many people have that same experience. Recordings for all the exercises were in production at the time this book went to print. Please check my website, www.bmindfulpdx.org, for the status of the recordings and how to obtain them.

Final Words

"The client is the Master. When the client knows what the Master knows, the client is healed."

–Bill Coulson

*"Vast is the heartmind of liberation,
A boundless field of benefaction."*

–first line, morning verse
Zen Center of Portland

The first quote is from one of my first mentors when I was training to be a client-centered therapist in the tradition of Carl Rogers. Bill was a senior student of Carl Rogers, and I found his words held wisdom for me as a psychotherapy client, a psychotherapist, and a student of Buddhism. Rogers advised us to really listen for the wisdom within the client and help them to know themselves. Similarly, the Buddha's advice is to work diligently and look at ourselves by focusing on parts (body, feelings, perceptions, mental contents) to be able to see clearly the whole, a mastery that already lies within us. This could be the most strategic and important offering of the Buddha.

The best advice I have for students is to consider that what you are looking for may lie within and to relax, be curious, and experiment with whatever you have come across in this book that seems like it might be a helpful tool in that self-inquiry. Trust yourself. You already know how to pay attention, in many ways. These exercises are intended to help attention be concentrated, clear, and free from clinging to this or that. The exercises you benefit most from are the one or ones you do frequently. Simply practice one thing until it is your own and it will be a tool you naturally reach for.

Probably the most common mistake I have made, and one I see with a lot of the students I work with, is the misunderstanding that what you are looking for is not within your reach RIGHT NOW! Mindful awareness is not far away and not only for those people who study Buddhism or live in monasteries. In this book you have read words like meditation, mindful awareness, ancient tradition, enlightenment, teacher, mastery, exercises, skills, and so forth. All of these concepts, this myriad of words, *are describing things that are difficult to put into words, so we think they are difficult to experience, but they are not.*

Awareness is always present, and being mindful of it is something you likely do often throughout your day but don't know "that was it!" Awareness is operating in the background all the time, like air, or like water in the background for fish. The knowledge that awareness is there for you all the time is another way to understand mindful awareness. It is simple, not complicated.

A friend said to me recently, "We do all this sitting practice to soften the constant thinking and see through to what is obviously already there." Noticing thinking when thinking, noticing feeling when feeling, noticing hearing when hearing. That is all there is to the practice and any reader can learn to do that. The heartmind of liberation (a heart and mind that are free to see, hear, feel what is really there) is always available to you. And when you access it, there is boundless benefaction available.

So, trust that you, too, can do this simple seeing, hearing, feeling and bring it into the practice we call Life. Ultimately, my wish for you is to live your life with attention that can recognize and be present to Life as it really is, with a heartmind that is free and knows how to love Life fully and not cling to any of it.

References and Notes

A Black Bag Strategy

1. Goldstein, J. (2013). *Mindfulness: A practical guide to awakening.* Boulder, CO : Sounds True, Inc.
2. Kabat-Zinn, J. (1993). *Full catastrophe living.* New York City, NY : Bantam Doubleday Dell Publishing Group.
3. Hanh, T. N. (1975). *The miracle of mindfulness: A manual on meditation (revised).* Boston, MA : Beacon.

Part I - The What and Why of Mindful Awareness

1. Young, S. (2011). *Five ways to know yourself: An introduction to basic mindfulness* An unpublished teaching manual. 7.
2. Lazar, S. (2005). Mindful Research. In C. Germer, R.Siegel, & P. R. Fulton. (Eds.). *Mindfulness and Psychotherapy.* New York City, NY : Guilford. 220-238.
3. Hanh, T. H. (1990). *Our Appointment with Life : The Buddha's Teaching on Living in the Present Moment.* Berkeley, CA: Parallax Press. 43.
4. Young, S. (2006). *What is flow?* An unpublished paper. http://www.shinzen.org/Retreat%20Reading/Flow.pdf
5. Young, S. (2011). *Five ways to know yourself: An introduction to basic mindfulness* An unpublished teaching manual. 61.

Part II - The How and Where of Mindful Awareness – The Contents of Your Toolkit

1. Lieberman, M.D., Eisenberger N.I., Crockett M.J., Tom S.M., Pfeifer J.H., Way, B.M. (2007). Putting feelings into words: Affect labeling disrupts amygdala activity in response to affective stimuli. *Psychological Science.* Vol 18/5, 421-428.
2. Young, S. (2011). *Five ways to know yourself: An introduction to basic mindfulness.* An unpublished teaching manual. 107.
3. See The significance of restful states, (2006) http://www.shinzen.org. For more information see Young, S., *Easy Rest: Reference Manual,* Young, S. (2008). http://www.shinzen.org.
4. Young S. (2011). *Five ways to know yourself: an introduction to basic mindfulness* An unpublished teaching manual. 35.
5. Hanson, R. (2009). *Buddha's Brain.* Oakland, CA: New Harbinger. 68. Marana, H.E. (2003). Our brain's negativity bias: Why our brains are more highly tuned to negative news. **Retrieved July, 2015** from *Psychology Today.*
6. Hanson, R. (2009). *Buddha's Brain.* Oakland, CA : New Harbinger, 68.
7. Fredrickson B. L., Levenson R. W. (1998). Positive emotions speed recovery for cardiovascular sequelae of negative emotions. *Cognition and Emotion.* 12:191-220; Fredrickson, B.L., (1998). What good are positive emotions? *Review of General Psychology.* 2:300-319.
8. To learn all of the Nurture Positive exercises see "The way of human goodness" in Young, S. (2011). *Five ways to know yourself: An introduction to basic mindfulness.* An unpublished teaching manual. 65-73.

Part III - There's an App for That! Applications of the Basic Mindfulness Toolkit

1. Hanh, T. N. (2009). *Happiness: Essential mindfulness practices.* Berkeley, CA : Parallax Press.
2. Young, S. (2013, January 5). Dharma talk. Lecture presented at year-end retreat in CA, Palos Verdes.
3. Lao Tzu, (2001). *The Book of the Way.* Berkeley, Los Angeles: University of Califonia Press).
4. Young, S. (2013, January 4). Dharma talk. Lecture presented at year-end retreat in CA, Palos Verdes.
5. Fronsdal, G. (2015). *Effort.* (Podcast 2/23/15).
6. Young, S. (2012, June 16). Home practice program. Lecture presented at Home Practice Program.
7. Examples of diagnosis-based mindfulness treatments are found in: Segal Z.V., Williams, J.M.G. & Teasdale, J.D. (Eds.). (2002). *Mindfulness-Based Cognitive Therapy for depression*; and Germer, C.K., Siegel, R.D., & Fulton, P.R. (Eds.) (2005). *Mindfulness and psychotherapy.*
8. Young, S. (2012, June 16). Home practice program. Lecture presented at Home Practice Program.

Part IV - Case Examples Using the Basic Mindfulness Toolkit

1. Tolle, E. (1999). *The Power of Now.* Novato : New World Library.
2. Young, S. (2012, June 16). Home practice program. Lecture presented at Home Practice Program.

Part V - Where Do I Go From Here?

MINDFULNESS TEACHERS AND TRAINING CENTERS:
- www.bmindfulpdx.org
- www.basicmindfulness.org
- www.shinzen.org
- www.centerformindfullearning.org
- www.modmind.org,
- www.mindsightinstitute.com

AUDIO DOWNLOADS, ARTICLES, BOOKS AND/OR WEB-BASED COURSES:
- www.soundstrue.com
- www.wisebrain.org
- http://www.positivityresonance.com/meditations.html
- http://www.self-compassion.org/01-Kristin-Neff-The-Self-Compassion-Break.mp3

GENERAL INFORMATION AND MEDITATION PREPARATION:
- http://www.thewayofmeditation.com.au/meditation-posture/
- http://www.dummies.com/how-to/content/preparing-for-meditation-sitting-still.html
- http://www.yogajournal.com/meditation/everything-need-know-meditation-posture/

9 780997 498004